INDIA

A guide to the experience

by David Stuart Ryan

Kozmik Press Centre
48A Astonville St, London SW18 5AL, UK
P.O. Box 42164, Washington DC 20015, USA

Contents

Author, David Stuart Ryan, has made three extended visits to the subcontinent. He studied Ancient History and Philosophy at King's College, London University, and has previously published a novel about the East – Looking for Kathmandu.

Editorial Consultants: Henry Kitchen and Elizabeth Debray.
Design: Peter Jacobsen
Production: Deryck Cheyne
Art Work: Paul Boyer
Copyright in all photographs: David Stuart Ryan except for those on pp 9, 56, 57, 58–9, 114, 115, 117, 122–3 and 128 which are copyright of Elizabeth Debray.
Public Relations: Lisa Norfolk

Front cover The pilgrims have left the bathing *ghats* of Benares, quiet has returned to the mighty Ganges river. In the darkness it is easy to feel the presence of all those who have come here to wash away their past in the ritual of renewal. Perfect peace.

India – a guide to the experience. First published by Kozmik Press Centre 1983. © David Stuart Ryan 1983.
Reprinted 1984

British CIP Data

Ryan, David Stuart
  India
  1. India
  954.05'2   DS407
  ISBN 0-905116-11-9
  ISBN 0-905116-10-0 Pbk

Library of Congress Cataloging in Publication Data

Ryan, David Stuart
  India: a guide to the experience
  1. India - Decription and travel - 1981   Guide books.
  I. Title
  DS414.2.R92 1983   915.4'0452   83-14921
  ISBN 0-905116-10-0
  ISBN 0-905116-11-9 Pbk.

Printed in Great Britain by
Whitstable Litho Ltd., Whitstable, Kent

Arrival – after the long dark night of India

The wind was blowing gale force at Heathrow airport when time came for departure. To see the grass rippling in the gusts like waves upon an ocean was reminder enough that we do indeed live at the bottom of a sea of air. It is an environment we have adjusted to so well that we hardly notice its existence. But 36 hours later, journey's end, sitting at dusk by the side of the Indian Ocean, drinking the local *feni* – a coconut brandy – the world seems an entirely benign place. The waves beat out a familiar tune, the air is rich and heady as it drives in from the seas, it is a joy to drink in the warmth and the gentle breeze. It is always good to return, and Kolva Beach has changed little in 15 years. We as a race have changed little from the days when our earliest ancestors came out of the sea onto the strange land. At night, caressed by the sea air, that decision, that prompting, is confirmed once again as having been exactly right.

But to reach this dawn of arrival must come first the dark night of the first day upon the great subcontinent. The most leisurely way to reach Goa's idyllic beaches from Bombay is to go by ship from the Bombay docks and arrive calmed 24 hours later. Most international flights arrive at dawn, well in time for the 10am ship departure. Or there is the train, wending its slow way through increasingly green and tropic countryside. Or there is the luxury bus (an ordinary coach by European standards). Or there is the plane. (Be sure to book it in advance). Finally there is the ordinary state bus. A mere 50 rupees will take you more than 200 miles south and give you an introduction to the 'real' India, if there is such.

The state bus's suspension appears to have long ago given up the ghost. A wise traveller would travel in the middle of the jolting frame. At the back of the vehicle every jolt is magnified as though you are sitting on a see-saw. As indeed you are. For the rear wheels finish two thirds of the way down the vehicle's body, leaving the tail to cavort (wildly) and throw its occupants unceremoniously up into the air, before crashing down with a bump on the hard wooden seats. Only to be thrown up into the air again at the next of the numerous pits in the road. Sixteen hours of this and the human frame has been catapulted into an altogether different, more hardened state, as is necessary for the rigours of the subcontinent where everything is on a grand scale. From the heights of experience to the depths.

In this bucking bronco of a night, thatched huts loom suddenly into view from their shrouding roadside trees, trees marked with white slashes of paint for the drivers of the quiet night roads. The trees are massive and profuse, entirely appropriate for a landmass which detached itself from Africa and then floated up to collide with Asia, creating the world's largest mountains in the resulting spectacular collision. Many of the hills are curved cones, testifying to ancient volcanic activity, the rivers have a great sweep to them, speaking of the vastnesses of the interior and the sheer scale of the land. India is wholly unique, its ancient origins having marked it out as a land in its own right that only very recently in geological history has become joined to a greater landmass. Recent indeed, the Himalayas are a mere two million years old, and are still being pushed inexorably upwards as the force of the impact with the Asian continent is absorbed.

Previous page The evening star appears above the palms of Goa, the sea disappears in a roseate glow, soon below a moonless sky there will be only the indistinct shapes of boulders, the rush of the breaking waves upon the sand and a feeling of space.

This dark dream of a night is a filmshow that delights and calls the deeper levels of a human being; the mind grapples to assimilate all these messages from the past as it heads for the soothing beat of a warm sea and reminders of from where we came.

The state bus set out from its Bombay terminal at 4.30pm. By 3am we are sitting in a *chai* shop deep in the interior. The occupants stir themselves to serve up sweet rich tea, while the eye is distracted by photographs of a naked man upon the walls. Closer examination reveals that the man is an adherent of an ascetic discipline that stems from far into the Hindu past when India was ruled by fear of avenging gods. By making *tapas* – penitence – he accrues merit for himself. The man in the photo has a perfectly proportioned upper body, which is marked with white daubs of horizontal paint showing his devotion to Shiva. But his contorted legs have withered away from lack of use, they are stick-like. His photograph has been adorned with a halo, people come to gaze upon his entirely naked form in awe while he looks back quietly and patiently, aware of the many thousands who have trodden this path of penitence before him. It is a tradition that owes nothing to the West.

Now, however, there are modern forms of penitence that we have despatched out into the world. It is the initiation the developed world gives to the shanty town dwellers who cluster on the fringes of the great modern cities. In a decade Bombay has swollen from some 4 million to nearly 10 million inhabitants, three quarters of whom live five to a room. The constantly arriving tribal people of the interior, and the agriculturally dispossessed, press in

Packed onto a causeway by the Arabian Sea, these shanty town dwellers in Bombay live in the shadow of the bustling commercial buildings of India's richest city. The children at least have the chance to expand out from the toehold their parents have gained – if they survive.

Previous page left The chill mist of dawn finds this *sadhu* already awake and waiting for the sunrise beside the Ganges. In the alcove where he has spent the night he keeps his bundle of possessions, while his food needs are taken care of by receiving alms.

Previous page right Morning in Benares. At the time of the monsoons in June to August the river can surge in height to near the very top of the steps, and increase its width from half a mile to nearly two miles as it floods the adjacent plains.

Fishing boats lie off Kolva's 40-mile-long beach, lined with perpetual palms. The tourists are swallowed up by the sheer vastness of the wide-open shoreline, for Kolva is still one of those places where the impact of nature is totally dominant.

on this already chronic overcrowding. Seeking some part of the city's wealth.

From a distance, Bombay is climbing white tower blocks, much like any other modern city. Closer to, the sprawling shanty towns, crammed onto any available space, become apparent. Dwellings are created from corrugated iron, palm fronds and mud walls, children play in the narrow lanes between the cramped huts, their mothers sweep out the family room with diligence, blissfully unaware that the open sewers and polluted water supply will take their inevitable toll in a few short years. But if the children live — life for most of the world is extremely hazardous in the first five years — then, yes, perhaps they will be able to take what the city has to offer; above all it offers the possibility of change.

Recognising instinctively, even gladly, that the old tribal ways must die, the children's parents have torn themselves away from the dark night of India. Perhaps they even recognise that they will, all too easily, become a sacrifice offered up to their children's success.

In India, Africa, South America, this is the way of the world we inhabit. If the present day poverty of the inhabitants seems savage from this distance, be sure that closer to those sewers and smells and ever-attendant diseases it is savage indeed. The survivors will remember what, if anything, was done to make their escape possible. Although we think of India as being a country of the past, it has a population who largely cannot remember before 1965 — when Kennedy and idealism were already put into suspended animation. For over 350 million Indians it is ancient history, so that it is our present response which is measured.

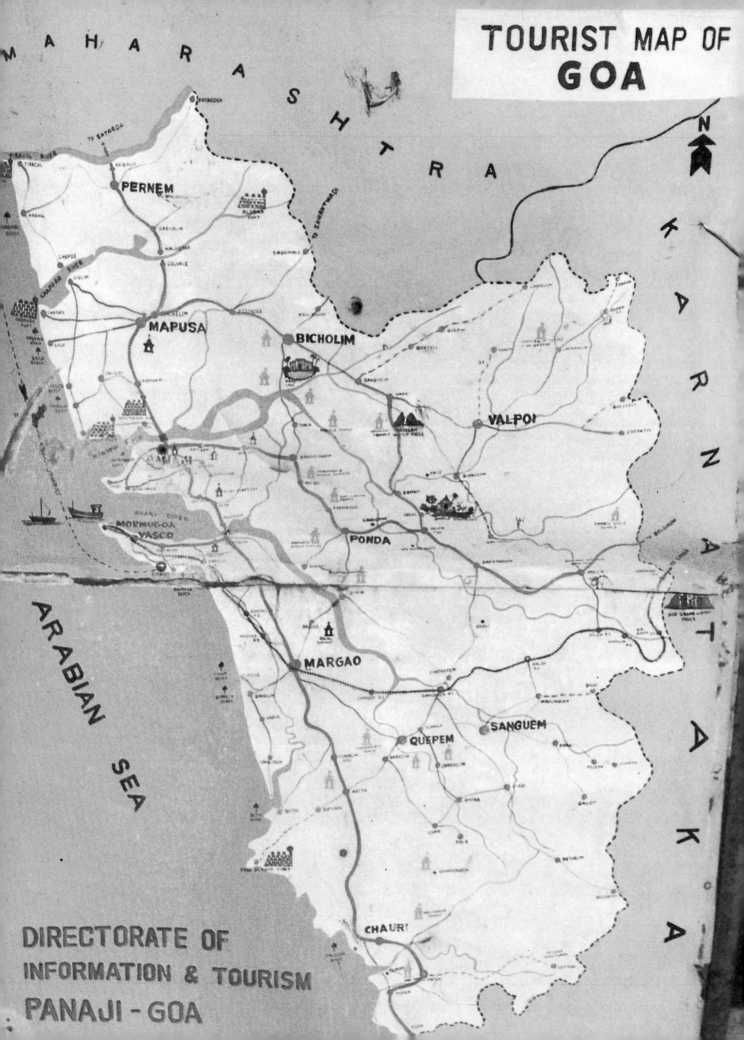

TOURIST MAP OF GOA

MAHARASHTRA

KARNATAKA

ARABIAN SEA

PERNEM

MAPUSA

BICHOLIM

VALPOI

VASCO
MORMUGOA

PONDA

MARGAO

QUEPEM

SANGUEM

CHAURI

DIRECTORATE OF
INFORMATION & TOURISM
PANAJI - GOA

Kolva beach – a touch of paradise

2

Kolva beach is approached along a winding road threading through fields (usually an intensely rich green) from the town of Margao. This is the first train stop if you come by rail from Bombay, and a place where you can make reservations for your departure, unless you are prepared to take a gamble on finding a seat (most unlikely).

Just ten years ago the road simply petered out into a cinder patch at the beach but now, by some wave of the Indian Tourist Board wand, there is a fully tarmaced space for buses and cars to turn, some modern hotels and tourist bungalows, a variety of restaurants. Kolva has become popular. But after the shock of acknowledging even favourite paradises have to move with the times, then it is relatively simple to extricate out the underlying harmony of what is still essentially a fishing village.

Come early in the morning and you will find only the bustle of the fishermen and women, sprinkling out the fish to dry in the already warm sun. During winter the temperature will reach 90°F by midday, getting hotter still until the monsoon storms arrive in June and July. Which is why most Europeans choose the period

Left Kolva beach looking south to the distant headland some 20 miles away. All along this white sandy beach is a line of palms that offers both shade and shelter. The fifth longest beach in the world, Kolva preserves its primaeval feel, nothing too much has changed.

Above Kolva's fishermen take in their net which is spread out in a huge semi-circle some 50 yards out into the sea and then hauled in with much exertion by a team of men heaving from each end. The sea shows no sign of exhaustion.

Previous page left A battered Tourist Board sign illustrates the main towns and beaches of Goa. Vagator, Baga and Calangute beaches are to be found to the north, the long straight sealine passing the town of Margao is Kolva. The capital, Panaji (Panjim), is partially obliterated by the seas' storms.

Previous page right Inhibitions tend to be lost 5,000 miles from home on an unspoilt, sun-warmed beach with the lure of the wide open sea reminding you that the body demands little more than to be exercised for it to give a feeling of well-being.

from October to March, though a few now stay all year round. The human body is infinitely adaptable.

Further along the beach, long lines of palm trees form a backdrop to the labours of men hauling in great circular nets that stretch out 50 yards into the sea. Slowly, the men drag back these nets and the trapped fish inside are rapidly sorted into piles; crabs and shrimps in one heap, small fish in another. The odd large stranger is tossed on whatever pile is nearest. So a great gaping-jawed monster, with lines of fine teeth, is still gasping its last breaths long after the silvery small fish have expired. To come close to the shore, is to run the increasing risk of being recruited into the food supply of a hungry India.

Now, many of Kolva's fishermen have motorised fishing boats and the catch has dramatically expanded. But along the thousands of miles of Indian coastline with its fine silky white beaches, the fishing industry has hardly begun to gather the riches that lie in the ocean.

As you enter the state of Goa, 'liberated' from 400 years of Portuguese rule in 1961, the landscape's colours change to the clean washes of blue and green that mark the southern shores of India. It is a tropical world and continues as such right down to the southern tip. These blues and greens perfectly complement each other, producing a calming effect that multiplies day after day until the rigours of travel in the dark interior of the subcontinent have been replaced by a certainty that here, at least, all is right with the world. Cats, dogs, goats, cows wander in and out of the palms by the shore, and in the actual village of Kolva which lies back half a

mile from the shoreline. Enter this village and the occasional dog may roar and yelp at intrusion into his closed world, but after the passing of a day or two you are recognised and magically no longer a stranger, but someone who belongs. A very satisfying feeling.

The truly unchanging Kolva is to be found north and south of where the road meets the ocean. Quickly, the shops and restaurants drop away and you are restored to the oldest juxtaposition of all, the one which has an undiminished hold upon us, the shoreline. And at Kolva this shoreline is the second longest in India, 40 miles of uninterrupted clean white sand which finally reaches distant blue mountains, even on a clear day they seem hazy and far off. For those who like to collect records, it is worth mentioning that there are only four longer beaches in all the world. Kolva has managed to stay true to its ancient self, the tiny cluster of shops, hotels and restaurants at the road notwithstanding.

Walk for fifteen minutes away from this cluster and you are restored to an elemental ocean meeting the palm-lined shore, peace, seclusion and an ancient rhythm that we still instinctively recognise. You can spend the day sheltering under a palm quietly contemplating this scene, or you can enter the always warm waters, which are blue, clear and joyous. To bathe in the sea has more than an element of ritual, of return. The brave creature who millions of years ago left comes back again. What has he learnt during his sojourn upon land? Was it worth all the extra thrills (and disappointments)? Only the dolphins could tell us, for they many millions of years ago returned from the land to the sea and have happily stayed, to be seen occasionally leaping out of the waters in playful *joie de vivre*.

Ah well, the choice for us was made. Late at night a great sea turtle comes upon the long Kolva shore to lay its eggs. It, too, returned to the seas some distant time ago. But this night the turtle expires upon the shoreline. By the next day, the birds have picked clean the cold, blubbery, flesh-covered form. During this night its flippers, worked by the waves into a simulacrum of life, make it appear a ghostly prophecy of the course of evolution, of our eventual success. It is we who gambled all on a better future. Such is the way to the stars, and perhaps a more lasting home than the earth's seas — in the scale of universal time.

The human creature who emerged from the oceans now has two very distinct forms as we realise once naked. The male all shoulders and slim hips, the female with that nipped in waist before the gracious curve of buttocks. Less suited for running fast, infinitely more comfortable to sit upon. Back in the sea the two forms merge as water glistens upon the skin, that slippery surface which has made us so well adjusted to the sea of air. A skin that demands to breathe and feel the air passing over it, just as some older tougher skin delighted in the wash of the sea. Time passes, seasons come and go, Kolva tells you. Its lessons are learned along the shimmering white beach with the very finest sand. Once upon its immensely long shoreline, the urge to return to the sea will become irresistible. Even for those who have not learnt to swim. Floating, the doubting mind is reminded that here we are still almost welcome. Not too much has changed, some instinct says. We have come a long way, and yet not so far. There is more to come.

Previous page One of the old boats that are to be found all along Kolva beach away from the village. They are built solidly enough for the summer storms. A 10-minute walk along the beach takes you away from the minor tourist development at Kolva.

3

The charmed circle of the village

Night by the seashore at Kolva is by no means the cessation of activity. Along the sealine, figures appear to float out of the dying, reddening light while they sort out the day's catch and begin the journey into town. Yet the ritual of death upon the sands has no aura of anguish, more of resignation, of this being how life has always fed upon itself. Rapidly the sun has dried out the tiny fish, and brought extinction to the gasping larger fish. The closing of night soon restores the shore to its pristine condition with only the beat of the white waves and the sea breeze interrupting the reverie of those who watch the going down of the sun from one of the beach bars which seem some odd parody of a Martini commerical, being no more than constructions of palms and odd pieces of wood, makeshift tables and chairs. 'Commercialisation' is a subjective description. As the sun approaches ever closer to the horizon, the Europeans become silent imperceptibly, it is not possible to be in Kolva and ignore this most dramatic event of the day.

In Kolva village the night brings an old closeness to the charmed circle. Even though many of the villagers rent out rooms to visitors, this has lost little of the intimacy of the settlement, they continue to live according to the old rhythms, it is the Europeans who adapt. It teems with the young of pigs, dogs and goats, has its own smells and sounds, is not disturbed by anything brighter than hurricane lamps and a few tiny bare bulbs. So dark is the village that it is always an effort to find one's hut, so different does the collection of palms and fields and bushes seem at midnight after listening to rock music under a tropic sky, and having drunk the native *feni*. Even old 'pros' who have lived in the village for months can be found in the early morning hours vainly searching for their huts, the feet have to know every part of the path to be sure of finding the way.

The village is entered off the road leading to Margao, some three or four hundred yards from the shore. Disappearing behind a large white orphanage the track takes you into a world where there is only the sound of snuffling pigs, and the low warning growl of dogs if they are approached too closely.

Great palms rise suddenly out of the ground, bushes snare the unwary leg, walls mark the edge of cultivated plots and are easily fallen over, it is as if you are entering the womb through the vaginal passage as the circle of the village opens out once the correct path has been taken, and within this circle all the old attitudes of life live on undisturbed. It is the group of approximately 200 who are able to live in harmony, a self-regulating group where each is known and tolerated. It conveys the eerie feeling of having come home.

Then on a near moonless night, the stars sparkle with a brightness that can only be seen in a tropical sky where the Plough hovers near the horizon. Even the starlight is clear enough to give a view of the thatched roofs and more solid walls of the huts, but they are a presence more felt than seen, giving off a palpable sense of security. The absence of the moon is felt most of all. It signifies the future bounty of a catch when the new moon arrives, for to observe the regular increase in catch at new and full moons is to become aware of why the fisherpeople give their first allegiance to

A fishing hut beside the sea. The night only interrupted by the steady beat of the breaking waves which foam white with their phosphoresence. Sudden storms can send the sea chasing up the beach with little or no warning, all in the morning is changed.

this heavenly body rather than the sun as we do in the West. But then the moon directly controls their fortunes through its rulership of the providing ocean.

Some one mile along the beach from the Kolva complex, there are fishermen who use oar-driven boats, rather than the newer motorised ones. They are still dressed as all the people on the beach were dressed ten years ago. Simply a silver chain slung around the waist, and a loin cloth of patterned pink drawn up over the crotch, revealing small firm buttocks, large swelling chests, strong muscular legs. Their 'modernised' fellow fishermen have

Previous page left After 3 months in Goa, the rigours of northern Europe have given way to a deep tan, a relaxed mood and a chance to think about the course of one's life. Will all the good resolutions melt away once back in the activity-dominated West? Perhaps not, in India it is possible to know freedom, an experience never quite forgotten.

Previous page right Children in India have to learn to make a living very early. This young pipe player in Chapora village has established a ready line in repartee and performance to bring in much valued *paisa* from the tourists.

Two fishermen, wearing the traditional silver belts and pink patterned loin cloths, laboriously heave their craft towards the sea over tarred blocks of wood. The weight of the boat necessitates that they are very fit. There are no out-of-condition fishermen here.

taken to wearing brightly coloured shirts and shorts, and have lost a little of their previous daunting fitness. Perhaps they have less respect for the powerful spirits of Kolva than the 'old fashioned' fishermen. The men in their loin cloths heave the boat towards the shoreline, sliding it over wooden blocks lubricated with black tar; it is a backbreaking task, for the boats are solidly built, as they must be to withstand the summer storms.

But it is not only the purist who will detect a greater independence in these men who rely utterly upon themselves, rather than worrying when the Indian government will next increase the taxes upon petrol. Every gain carries some loss.

The fine powdery texture of the sand is amply demonstrated by a footprint, Kolva is a pristine beach where sea turtles still come to lay their eggs, as they undoubtedly have for millions of year. The Indian government shows a praiseworthy concern for its treasure of wildlife.

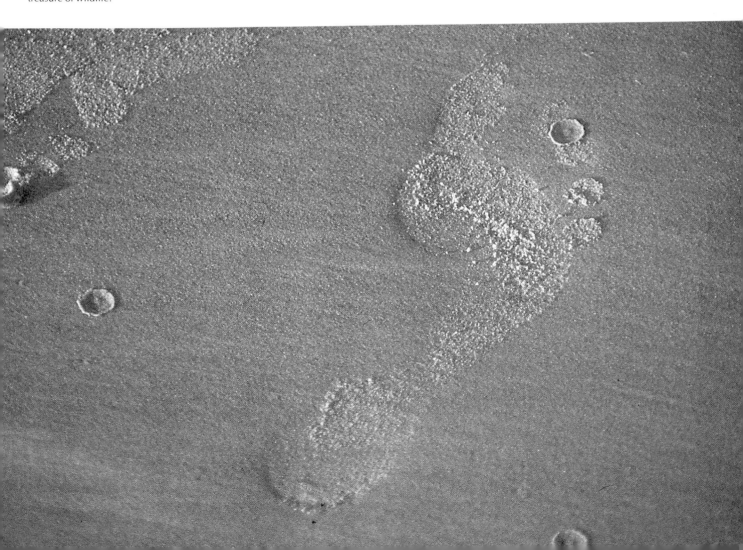

4 Dreams

Opposite In the dying rays of the sun a Frenchwoman dresses, after a day of sunshine, for the evening party at Vagator beach. In fairy tale colours and landscape, the Europeans quickly get into the habit of celebration and there are many large rented houses where the parties are held.

Against a backdrop of the ever present palms, a young *sadhu* – Harepit Maharaj – walks across Vagator beach with his German girlfriend. This is how he travels all over India, sleeping among the trees, and certainly appears to be perfectly pleased with his life.

'We look in amazement at these people, and ask ourselves, could they ever have ruled us?' It is a 65-year-old Goan speaking, who has spent some five years in West Germany. He is unable to equate the former stiff rulers of his country with the sun-loving casual young who now flock to Goa's beaches. He can date the time of the explosion of interest very exactly. The 1967 British Overseas Airways calender featured paradises around the world, and one spot chosen was the old Portuguese colony of Goa. Now, a decade and a half later, there are literally thousands of Europeans to be found in Goa. The most popular beach is Calangute, near to the capital of Panjim, and during the last few years a small service industry has grown up to cater for the tourists as they are now called unselfconsciously. Tourism has become Goa's major industry, just as it is about to become for the whole of India, with forecasts that by 1990 the present thousands of visitors – particularly in the winter months – will have become tens of thousands. However, with the sheer numbers of Indians, the Europeans will never alter the fundamental character of the country. The old *sahibs* have simply metamorphosed into affluent sun-worshipping *bon viveurs*. They continue to live separate lives from the 'natives'.

There are half a dozen superb beaches in Goa, each with its

own band of enthusiasts. Kolva is one of the most southerly; moving north come Calangute, Baga, Anjuna and Vagator beaches, each that little bit more remote from prying Indian eyes than the last – and proportionately less 'developed'. Calangute has as many home comforts as a Greek Island, with superb restaurants by Indian standards at least, and a huge variety of hotels.

At Vagator beach, you are very close to the natural world, with simple huts along the back of the beach dispensing tea and Indian meals, while above the beach towers a hillside populated with palms and little else. At the top of the hillside you have to walk several miles to reach either Anjuna village or Chapora village.

A picture of Krishna incarnate emerges from the palm trees at the foot of the hillside which protects Vagator beach from all but the most determined Indian middle-class voyeurs. The Europeans tend to act as if they are in the South of France, remaining unmoved by the puritanical attitude to sex of modern Indians. But the man who has emerged from the palms of the hillside is not a modern. His hair is long and loose, burnished with many sun-lightened streaks. He wears a deep red *dhoti* around his waist, carries a small bundle in his hand together with a shining brass bowl. Accompanying him is a young European woman. She is approximately 22, he about the same age. His body is tall and in perfect shape, his face wide open and handsome, in fact flashing with vitality. The girl has dark long hair, neatly tied into a long pigtail. She gets up from the spot on the beach where she and her Indian companion have stopped and returns to the gap in the palms from which they emerged, now

There are many pre-school-age children to be found on Goa's beaches. Their parents have often set up residence for some months, as houses can be rented for approximately £25 a month. The best buys are now permanently rented.

carrying one of the brass bowls to fill it with water. She is barefoot, with a sheath of a dress of thin cotton held in place by a belt. The dress has no sides, being simply a strip of material with a gap for the head. Through these open sides her exceptionally well-proportioned body can be seen. Closer to the girl, you become aware of her eyes that sparkle with light and delight in the day. The young *sadhu* – holyman wanderer – places his three-pronged rod – symbol of Shiva, dissolver and creator in the Hindu trinity – in the sand. The young European girl returns with the water. She must have kitted out the *sadhu* with his new red *dhoti*, and new brass bowls; these it appears are their only requirements. You do not need to be told they have slept out in the palms, they carry all the harmony of the natural world with them.

No, he does not want his photograph taken, and unlike most objectors you have to take this refusal seriously. There is no threat, simply that you do not want to lose his good wishes.

His girl companion will, no doubt, eventually return to the West, to the German economic miracle, but it is easy to see in India what appeal this handsome, perfectly healthy, sure male has. He is living according to beliefs that long predate Christianity. For Hinduism is at once sophisticated and also rooted in the simplicities of nature's life cycle. It is tolerant of variations upon its all-embracing philosophy and with its ability to enfold an unbeliever it has survived many cultural invasions intact. For present-day Westerners, living in a void, it is immensely seductive.

The idyllic picture of the red-clothed *sadhu*, his Shiva rod planted in the sand, with his faithful consort is interrupted by some woman friends of the German girl joining them on the beach to watch the sunset. The young *sadhu* is more obviously visiting a European enclave in India, as Goa has been for nearly all the last 400 years.

And yet, and yet, as the sun sets outlining palms, burning a deeper and deeper orange, it is not the *sadhu* who has left his home in the world of the subcontinent, it is the Europeans who have come to join him here as he follows the dictates of his heart, who have come to know freedom, to let the laws happen, to participate in the inevitable evolution of the world.

Darkness comes, the people retire to cafés and restaurants to listen to music – Indian music with its constantly changing and charging rhythms.

The night

5

Left The daughter of one of the beach cafe proprietors at Vagator beach. He has four children and entirely depends on the tourist trade in winter to make a living. Such impermanence might be judged anxiety-producing in the West, but the man has a typically Indian philosophical attitude towards his future.

Walk between Vagator beach and Chapora village and you enter an entirely dark natural world with great palms towering above. Suddenly out of the darkness lights gleam, in this case an isolated restaurant which still, by Goan standards, prospers with the influx of tourists.

Night-time in India. On a thin strip of tarmaced road, feet make a familiar pat. But all else is different. Heading for the village of Chapora from Vagator beach under a brilliantly star-lit sky. At the edge of the road, the shapes of great palms and trees rise impenetrably, for without the moon it is extremely dark, with only the rustles of unseen pigs, dogs and rats out there in the murk. There is a perfect palpable silence which gives emphasis to the dimly perceived great sweep of the earth under the sky, a dark unchanging presence. There is no threat of human violence as would be the case in much of the West. Perhaps the natural world contains a few terrors but in the warmth of the night slowly walking with a companion it is possible to feel a part of the world, and to feel that is enough, the sense of belonging is a warm one. Eventually the distant lights of Chapora village show through the intensely dark trees, feet grope along the trail, and you enter a human world from out of some jungle fantasy, hurricane lit shops selling bananas, cheap teas, lazily stirring in the cool of the evening, it seems strange after the quietness of the road and tracks to be once again surrounded by human kind.

Back at the sea shore it was the elemental world. The openness of the seascape allows the light of the stars to vaguely pick out grey shapes of rocks on the wave swept sand. The noise of the sea is

immediately realised to be infinitely powerful, the real underlying strength by which all else is measured. Clambering over these rocky shapes, jumping to the sand, the sea rushing noisily between gaps in the rocks, a stretch of flat sand, a view of the dark immensity of the ocean, then more rocks to be carefully clambered over, feet moving faster than the vision opens up the way, scaling the steeply rising hillside at Vagator beach leading to a café where the Europeans gather before proceeding to a party.

The village people from Chapora and roundabout gather at the approaches to a house some long-term European visitors have rented for £25 a month. It is large, with its own gardens. Squatting down with hurricane lamps to light the wares they sell, the Indian villagers look upon the guests with the quiet appreciation of those who know they will remain on the outside, as at some Maharajah's *durbar*. They sit beside their piles of cakes, their brewing tea, their jewellery, with an infinite patience, grateful that they can earn more from a few casual sales than a week's toil in the fields can produce.

Word of a party always spreads at great speed among the Europeans, there are the motorbike taxis whose riders quickly learn of the whereabouts of a celebration. Some Europeans stay for 6 months and more and appreciate the chance of giving hospitality, it is the perfect recipe for instant communication. Moreover, it is not completely removed from the old British Raj way of life. The customs are as equally bizarre to the all-seeing villagers. The land is filled for miles around with the steady thump of amplified rock music, while the guests dance, sit and chatter in groups. An order for tea is inexplicably delivered by villagers who appear to have total recall of faces, and where their customer may be found. They are exceptionally trusting if, as often happens, they cannot change more than the smallest notes and ask you to return when you have broken down a 10 rupee note into singles. Change is always short outside the cities. It is well to remember that a 100 rupee note, the rough equivalent of a £10 note, represents nearly a month's wages for many of these people.

Night in India is all black shadows off the few roads, it is a country that has to be felt physically. Lights, when they do appear, seem dazzling in their intensity, even if they are a few bulbs outside a simple house.

It is the true India, increasingly interrupted by the roar of motor cycles and their probing headlights. Affluence is coming to some of those in the villages, the India of criss-crossing motorways cannot be much further behind. Most likely, the intersecting pathways and roadways that have carried travellers for much of time will become motorised slowly, but now it is still possible to walk the highways undisturbed as in a mediaeval existence with villages suddenly discovered, and with them food, light and warmth.

22-year-old Hanna from Hamburg, a cabinet maker by trade, who has spent 3 months travelling around India by herself. For her, the true India is to be found in the interior, walking along the quiet roads under the brilliant stars.

And just as the land reveals its secrets in the dark of a germinating new moon, so it is by the seashore where the gradual wearing down of the dimly outlined rocks can be sensed much more than it can be seen. Above all, the creation, the star filled sky, perfectly bright stars in perfectly clear air. A place to breath in deeply with nothing to disturb, a welcome warmth in the air, pollution still a problem for the future.

The sheer health and vitality of the man striding to the beachside cafes radiates out from this picture. It is necessary, but also very easy, to get fit and full of an inner glow in Goa, the ultimate argument for a visit.

The vagaries of the human body

6

Name: Harepit Maharaj. Sometimes to be found in Hardwar, sometimes in Rishikesh, on the upper parts of the Ganges river as it plunges down from the Himalayas. Rishikesh has a steady flow of visitors coming to seek Indian wisdom, and has done ever since the time of the Beatles. But the ashrams which give lectures there cannot match the meeting of a genuine *sadhu* who is more content to wander than live in some cleansed version of the old Indian teaching schools. Learning is best achieved through emulation, you realise, contemplating the wiry strength of the young *sadhu*'s body.

'But I have no address,' he laughs, uproariously, pleased at the contradiction.

His German girlfriend smiles at this boyish good humour, he feeds a puppy through the teat of a baby's bottle, constantly massaging the pup which is filled with obvious delight. Behind his head the sunset burns orange.

'I have no doubts in my God,' the young man goes on, still playing with the pup, still filling his consort's eyes with amused admiration. 'He gives me everything.'

You consider the filled fruit bowl he is eating from, have to agree. He radiates good health, good humour. There is the dust of many hundreds of miles of Indian roads upon him, and the slow village lifestyle. You realise that he knows the jungle, its creatures, its fruits, it's habits, at every time of the day and night. There are no terrors in the world.

Sitting in this beachside restaurant, some few yards up the sloping hillside of Vagator, in the presence of a man who knows India's land intimately, the rhythm of the earth, the coming and going of the sun, is felt to be all important, the only spectacle worth watching. It is the steady accompaniment of our forays out into space and time, and when the foray has finished, then must come the return to the underlying harmony.

The mind, ever curious, wonders if perhaps yes, this 'Maharaj' is just that.

He has the looks, the confidence, the at-oneness to be a prince. And was not the Buddha a prince who went out into the world? You reject the idea and still wonder. As the night closes, Harepit Maharaj and his young woman go off, to their spot by the sea, to be wrapped in a thin blanket, to await the coming day. To enjoy the world, it is necessary to be tough as well as open.

The view at the commencement of day from the rocks and sheltered cove of Vagator beach is all mountains and sun, sand and water, with just a few Europeans to be spotted in their tents on the hillside. The sea is already warm and an early morning swim brings the body vibrantly awake, instead of being forgotten the superb machine thrills you with its own vitality, the ever present Western doubts, fears of the future, are put to sleep by the body's affirmation of life.

The middle of the day. There are a few swimmers lazily basking in the water. The temperature is in the 90°F range. On the beach there are bodies rapidly browning, no signs of movement beside the occasional shift of position of a naked torso. An Indian ear cleaner moves along the beach seeking custom, as he passes from group to group. With delicate care he probes inside the ear to find

Opposite Originally from Rajasthan, 26-year-old Ekbal has learnt 19 languages by moving around India and listening intently to each regional language spoken by the local people. There are 14 major languages in India.

Previous page The rite of sunset, the passing of time, the meditation upon the revolving world, all activity stops for the coming of night once you are back in the natural world. Pollution, change, lie somewhere over the horizon.

One of the attractions of secluded Vagator beach is a stream which runs down the wooded hillside. The girl has just finished washing the salt from her hair. Most Europeans cannot resist gaining an all-over tan in these seductive surroundings.

the balls of accumulated wax, many Europeans cannot believe how much wax these *kan-saf wallas* are capable of removing. But no, it is the residue of years of neglect. For little more than the price of a ball of cotton wool, the hearing can be restored to its former clarity. The lap of the sea seems louder, far-off noises come clearly through the air. There is a message of hope in India's concern for the physical body, and its undreamt of powers of self-renewal. For all their avowed interest in materialism, the Westerners confuse their belief in an image of themselves with the reality of their bodies. Hardly believing that they do in fact exist in the physical world. How else do you explain the punishment handed out to the body?

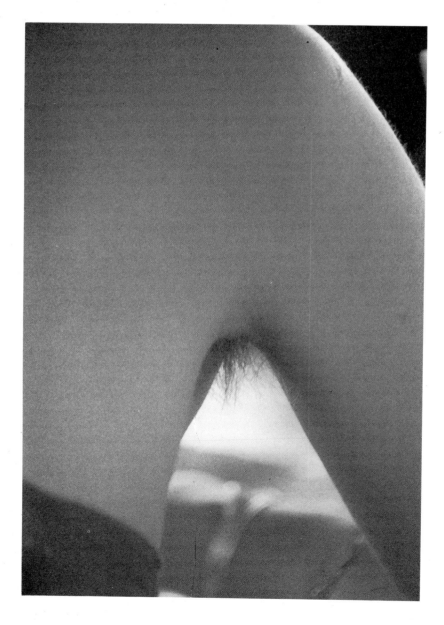

Women in India quickly adopt the brightly coloured materials and bracelets of the people. Indeed there is now a busy trade in many things Oriental in the West, but to become a successful importer needs a good background knowledge — and above all outlets for the merchandise.

There is a huge variety of fresh fruit to be found in semi-tropical Goa and the tourist influx has enabled people who earn only £10 a month on average to supplement their income by walking along the beach with their wares. It is all done with the maximum of Goan friendliness.

The masseur has studied the vagaries of the human body under the guidance of a *guru* in the art of being a masseur. He spent three months at an ashram in Bombay. With a surprising strength his fingers dig into the muscles of the body, unknotting blockages, relieving the tenseness, restoring the underlying wholeness. The massage is savage, the head is wrenched to the side with a click, the fingers and toes are yanked out of their sockets with a loud snap, but then a feeling of relaxation overcomes the discomfort of being stretched and some centering agency within revels in the harmony.

The heat of an Indian winter quickly peels off reddened skin. But the masseur has an answer for that too — soothing coconut oil. After a week the temperature seems entirely normal, the European winter has become a memory, it is a time for exuberance, a celebration of health. The first lessons we learnt are the easiest to forget, and must be repeated periodically.

The unhurried pace of a day

All day and all night by the sea at Vagator, what can one learn at such close proximity? A white sleeping bag is marooned on the sand, further back from the beach dogs stir; they growled ferociously at the European intruders who came at the dead of night with their probing torchlights searching for a spot to sleep. Perhaps unaware that there had been a scare on the beaches of Goa when a deranged European (rumoured to be Czechoslovakian) had taken an axe to three people sleeping upon the tropic beach and killed them. A scare would be an understatement. The murders had taken place on a remote beach near to Chapora village, after the killings there were no odd seekers of enlightenment through communion with nature, at least on that beach. But time quickly heals.

On Vagator beach, by nine in the morning, there are a dozen Europeans gathering at the cliffside stream that gently trickles down to the beach and offers some relief from the salt that stays long after the sea water has gone. No matter, it is still heavenly to be able to wash in such an uncluttered, unspoilt place. Comforting rumours of the arrest of the Czechoslovak calm the itinerants, even though the rumours are false and have merely resulted in increased police surveillance of the expatriate community.

Some of whom quite definitely have something to hide, like this man from Northern Ireland, who answers no questions, only betrays his violent heritage in his accent, who speaks of strange religious sects who go about their business in a particularly vicious way. In Bengal, a group of these *Ananda Marg* followers were ambushed by the Communists, the Northern Ireland exile explains, 'They were cut to shreds with machetes.'

A young English boy of about five, naked, is surrounded by a group of Indian day trippers. He retreats, querulous. The separation of the countries and the cultures is brought home, there is an aggressiveness in the Indians' curiosity.

As the day moves on from the serenity of morning, more people arrive on the beach from various nearby parts including the villages of Chapora and Anjuna, for Vagator is simply a beach, with no village beside it. It can only be reached by a long walk. This helps to explain the camaraderie of the Europeans here, they meet over breakfast, and then spend the rest of the day smoking, talking, swimming, lazing, sunbathing. Native girls come past carrying heavy baskets of fruit. If you buy, you must help the girl to get the basket back upon her head, while she is mildly disturbed that her customer is naked, yet does not think that the male form will appreciate her, not that she would expose herself upon the beach, tradition is too strong for that.

The waves slowly retreat as the day wears on. Other Europeans upon the beach, in small groups and individually, use the odd request for a light, or the use of suntan lotion to engage in conversation. Rote questions pale into insignificance beside the reality of a body breathing in the heady air coming off the sea. Name of home town, of country, even of self, mean little in comparison to being utterly at ease in a friendly environment. The economist from northern Norway is lying back on her arms, then rising to curl her legs underneath her buttocks. A first contact is made, we begin to talk, the wind glides over the skin, the link that

Opposite top The early morning sun dispels the mist which gathers in the fields behind Kolva beach. There is a chill in the air during December and January at night, but by March the sand gets too hot to walk on at mid-day.

Opposite bottom For anyone who is fascinated by wildlife, and birds in particular, there is a magnificent profusion of species to study. Eagles hover over mountains and rivers, vultures pick at their prey, parrots fly through the upper branches of trees, in a magnificent profusion of tropical colour.

comes from being European in an exotic clime is made the more fascinating by the differences, the curves of the breast, the clump of unattended hair, — briefly the pink of the lips opening as she rises to leave after having been perfectly at ease in the resfreshing air, with the sense of confidence that comes from being who you are, if ever so briefly.

At night, there is another party. People from a dozen countries gather, they wander about the grounds of the house, dance, talk, watch. Mostly they sit and watch. But the sea is just beyond the grounds of the house. It calls with the dark waves briefly foaming white. You look out to this sight, eventually go to be near the ocean and feel the stars above more closely, unable to properly communicate with another human being, reduced as you are to awe and wonder by the black backdrop of the ocean and the sky beyond. The girl is perfectly silhouetted against the stars. It is a question of us deciding when we are ready to attempt communion with the powers hinted at in the light of the stars of night.

In India, it is always a continental-sized view, or celebration, or history. And that includes the tragedies. Every year some visitors are lost. Lost down the wells that dot the dark earth, and are necessarily very deep, lost into the waves of the deceptively simple sea, lost to the bites of snakes, (8,000 a year die in India from snakebites, as many as from road fatalities in England), lost to the sudden mysterious diseases that lie in wait for all those who allow themselves to become run down. Some disappear from choice, like the Irishman who you instinctively realised does not welcome questions. Who has the deep brown look of one who has spent a whole year or more in India. How many did he maim? You wonder.

Further south, the villages get sleepier still among their ever attendant palms. The backwaters of Kerala hiding a multitude of animal life. The hill resort of Ooty in Tamil Nadu at 7,000 feet, the retreat of the old British administrators during the time of the Raj, the beautiful botanical gardens of the Theosophical Society in Madras with the world's largest banyan tree. The south, and this includes Goa, is a lazy dream, only interrupted by the storms of the summer season, it slows the body and the mind, it relaxes and it prepares for the onslaught upon the senses that is the populous India of the Ganges plains to the north.

Yet written upon the faces of the Goans are the marks of many memorable storms. Those seeking the perfect undisturbed paradise must seek elsewhere.

Opposite Work begins at dawn for this young Goan woman who cultivates the lush fields which stretch back from Kolva beach. Traces of her Portuguese heritage can be detected in the round face and strong body, also the extrovert smile.

The process of change

8

The coastline of southern India has seen many visitors from other shores over more than 2,000 years. There are records of the Romans and the Greeks trading with the Indian subcontinent, led on by the lure of pepper, silks, precious stones and rich perfumes. In the hills of Goa are many precious and semi-precious stones, while in the Himalayan peaks of Kashmir are truly fabulous gems which the Kashmiris have a justifiable reputation for working into glorious artifacts. Kashmir, too, is near the old Chinese caravan route – the Silk Road now haunted by abandoned cities – which over a period of years took the merchants across central Asia until they reached the Roman Empire's outposts.

So the unchanging slowness and regularity of life in the south, with its long trail of white beaches and palms, is something of an illusion. As is the lusciousness of the vegetation; in Kerala you will find village children with little to eat, living in squalid dirt.

The overall and true mood of the south is that of the tropics, of vivid sense impressions whether of sight, smell or sound. It is a very physical environment that cannot be hermetically sealed away. Even though there are exclusive beach resorts such as the Fort Aguada Beach Resort in Aguada, Goa, where 5-star Western comfort can be purchased for 400 rupees (£25) a day.

For 400 years Goa gradually took on a Portuguese character, but since the 1961 'liberation' more and more Indians from neighbouring states have come to this former enclave with its fertile soil and booming tourist trade that is rich by Indian standards, for in India a man can work an hour to earn 15 pence, and live on 30p a day.

However, Goa always was India. The Christian churches never converted more than a minority of the native inhabitants. At Chapora village, away from the Portuguese-founded large towns, there are only Hindu shrines and temples. Along the dark road, an impressively large temple appears, testimony of the still strong Indian devotion to their gods. For this is a new temple, built by the villagers in gratitude for the wealth their Western visitors are bringing.

This Hinduism also means that Goa, like the rest of India, is one gigantic farmyard, where a sacred cow or a goat will calmly walk up to a restaurant table and scoff its contents before the astonished diners' eyes, where the litters of piglets, puppies and kittens are all allowed to survive although they are unaided and must take their chances along with the human population. As the *sadhus* prove, the land is fruitful enough, the weather mild enough, to let a truly simple man wander at will and still escape desperate want.

But it requires a simplicity we in the West lost in the Middle Ages and again in our early childhood. It can only be re-acquired by Westerners sated with material abundance.

Chapora village is an uneasy compromise between, on the one hand, the sophistication of the incoming tourists and, on the other, the basic simplicity of the villagers. So tourist eating houses have multiplied with a great variety of foodstuffs, and there are now a handsome clutch of motorcycles, many acting as taxis. Fortunately, their riders have not adopted Western speeding techniques, which would be disastrous on roads where a cow may be sleeping, or village women chattering. However, the peace of Chapora is being lost, and with that loss perhaps it is inevitable that there will

Opposite An old woman smokes a *bidee* cigarette, hand-rolled from local grasses. If you are able to acquire a taste for the pungent aroma, a packet of 30 *bidee* cigarettes will cost you 50 *paisa*, about 7 pence.

Although most Goans are Hindus, there is a strong Christian presence. Roadside shrines suddenly gain candles at sunset. But because this is India it is the holy spirit, the ignored member of the Trinity moving in mysterious ways, who receives the most worship.

be an eroding of the old beliefs and certitudes to be replaced by a fear of what the future may bring. As has already happened in the West.

So Chapora, like the rest of India, enters a period of rapid change — an opportunity for those who can adapt fastest. For people like Ekbal Soyet, from Rajasthan in India's desert-covered North West. At 26, he can speak 19 languages, most of the Indian languages and those of the tourists. He talks to the visitors and learns their language in the same way he learnt those of the Indian states, he has an acute ear and a lightning quick mind. He is married to a partially crippled woman back home and looks after their child by sending back money from what he earns acting as a guide to the tourists, migrating with them from Goa to Bombay as the weather heats up and drives all but the hardiest of the Europeans further north.

As the migration begins, Europeans renew the long leases on their houses for another year. People like the famous 8-finger Eddie who has been returning to Goa each year for 15 years. He looks surprisingly untired by the harshness of the Indian summer climate. But then, he retires up Kathmandu in the Himalayas during the monsoons and to Benares on the Ganges in the autumn. Just as the rulers of the Raj migrated to the hills for the blast of summer. By May, before the monsoon breaks, the temperature can soar to a spectacular 120°F, so hot that even the Indians die from the heat. After a party, it will be time to leave the green land and white beaches of Goa for another year.

The menu in the more enterprising Indian restaurants and cafes features many of the tourists' favourite foods: fried eggs, porridge, toast and jam, pancakes. For those who want to eat Indian style, a good meal can be had for 20 pence.

The strange interlude of night

9

The boat from Panjim to Bombay, 250 miles to the north, takes a leisurely 24 hours and departs at 10am from the Panjim docks where a ticket is bought for either the upper or lower decks (the upper being preferable) and then a mad rush ensues to find a place to spend the next 24 hours in comfort. Porters will, for a few rupees consideration, hurry onto the boat ahead of the baggage-laden crowd, and dutifully find a spot for their customer. You pray it is not near one of the lavatories.

The boat calls at exotic sounding ports along the way – Bankot, Ratnagiri, Dapoli. Passengers are ferried out aboard huge rowing boats from isolated palm-hidden townships. By the time dusk closes rapidly in, you have soaked in the tropic coast atmosphere of sheer laziness and desuetude, at the same time marvelling at the unreality of places that are seen as a few lights and bulky shadows out there in the darkness of the insect-heralded night.

Bombay seen from the approaching Goa boat, which takes a leisurely 24 hours to sail the 250 miles. The first indelible impression of Bombay is the rich aroma that unmistakeably tells you that you are in a very different place where all previous judgements must be temporarily suspended if you are to understand.

A boy selling peacock feathers on a Bombay street. In this bustling town there are pedlars of every service and commodity. The shops in Bombay sell excellent native crafts and at little more (if you bargain) than in the villages and towns 'up station'. You need to gain a fair idea of quality and the usual price before buying; take your time, the Indians will.

By 10pm all the Indian passengers, who are used to retiring shortly after nightfall, have ingeniously found themselves some space upon the cramped decks and wooden benches, never protesting at what their fellow passengers do, but retiring into their own private world. Very necessary in a country where privacy is virtually unknown. It is a rare opportunity to see that the Indian women actually do huddle close to their men, after all day keeping a studied distance and indifference. Now the intimacy of family life is briefly revealed, as the strangeness of a journey interrupts the familiar flow and restrictions of their life.

A group of young Indians, lit by one lamplight on the deck, gather together to sing remarkably harmoniously their favourite songs from the Indian films that dominate the popular consciousness. Disco dancing, and disco music is the latest vogue. The Indian youths quickly join in with their own traditions of community song and spontaneity. The tribal life of India is still close to the surface, even though the youths all wear Western trousers and shirts.

In the fetid atmosphere of the ship's restaurant, a pair of Westerners play bridge with an Arab on holiday from Saudi Arabia. The strain of concentration in the extremely humid night produces beads of perspiration upon his forehead as he sees his opponents come from behind to win the 11 tricks they promised. Eventually even they make their way to the deck beside the ship's benches and fall into a slumber in their sleeping bags dreaming to the dreams of Indian film music.

The first signs of dawn find the Indians rising, as if in a mass, and methodically going to wash their mouths out and splash water over themselves at the deck fountains. Quickly they become animated while the brilliant red sunset that saw in the night has now changed to a pale orange spreading out across a perfectly calm sea. The sun is seen through mists while, with increasing frequency, ships come into view announcing the closing proximity of the great port of Bombay, long a British settlement that during the 19th century became the focus for India's trade with overseas.

The white towers of the office blocks and the apartment blocks rise on the horizon. Closer in, you are still unable to see the thousands who sleep upon the streets, to smell the hundred rich rancid aromas that immediately impinge themselves upon the senses of any new arrival.

Night time in the Grant Road area of Bombay. A great cacophony of battered cars, taxis, lorries, buses and bikes. The drivers are unable to drive without hooting incessantly, as if announcing their presence. It is every driver for himself, as cars thread in and out, honking, braking, squeaking into spaces, miraculously not colliding. Off the Grant Road, girls are lined up for the inspection of the passers-by, as brazen as the whores of any city they hiss excitedly to prospects or make very explicit signs with their fingers and hands. The smell of open sewers, the dust, the petrol fumes, the humidity, the noise, prevent the backdrop of old wooden houses from looking merely picturesque. The reality of young women sinking into this most faded of faded dreams is all too obvious. It is a street of poor pleasures for the not quite so poor. An 18th century part of town where those in the 19th century and early 20th can come to satisfy errant desire. Five rupees for five minutes. Tucked away among the prostitutes' rooms are opium dens where you can find battered Europeans slumped against walls, oblivious to the squalor all around, while the room's proprietor dutifully counts great wads of small notes. If ever there was an apt phrase, grubbing for money describes the opium trader's business.

Bombay spreads out geometrically in all directions producing a great swirl of tattered and makeshift buildings here in its poor quarters. The official estimate for the population is some 8 million, having grown from 1 million at the time of independence in 1947. But add the armies of the destitute, the shanty camp dwellers, the transients and 10 million would be a more accurate figure. Yet still the thousands pour into India's busiest, most prosperous, most Westernised city.

In Bombay everything has a price, and everyone is trying to sell something. Is it the way all India has to go?

Opposite Two of the estimated 30,000 prostitutes to be found in the Grant Road area of Bombay. At night the streets are alive with the bustle of men, by day they return to their true identity as one of the poorest areas of town, preyed upon by those who are in any way richer.

A crumbling archway is the entrance to a lane in old Bombay where a busy army of men are engaged in their own trade. Rather like mediaeval London, each lane is devoted to a particular trade, although the repairers of 20th century transistorised circuits are also to be found here.

The great rush forward

10

Walk along Marine Drive, Bombay, a great sweep of a road lining the Arabian Sea, and you will happen upon many of the world's more eccentric travelling showmen. An Indian has to use his wits to survive, his act has to be good, while with life led on the streets he can be sure of an instant audience.

So you are regaled by a man carrying two cobras in an innocuous basket. At a call from his pipe they ominously rise and extend the flaps behind their heads and very beady eyes. On the other side of the road you meet a young boy with a monkey on a lead, and for a small consideration the boy will get his monkey to do lifelike impressions of a baton-wielding policeman. The show is good and the demands for payments of perhaps 20 rupees are insistent and massively overpriced. In Bombay you have to quickly develop a very firm line in refusal, in reckoning what a service is worth and paying only that for it. This is not to say that you should join in the ruthless exploitation of the poor, simply that with so many demands for money it helps to have some idea what an importuner of services really expects. Distasteful as the average European may find bartering, in the East it is a ancient, long practised custom.

Beggars without legs jet-propel themselves across the road on small wheeled carts in defiance of the rush of oncoming traffic, with no driver prepared to give way to anyone else. One spectacular cart driver applies hand held wooden blocks to the road as he just crosses to the far side in time. Life is a constant drama in this great swirling city.

Old Bombay. The houses are made of wood, and lean crazily in all directions. All about are open stalls selling the recycled scrap of more affluent societies. Here nothing is thrown away. The pathways are thronged with people. A beggar – more accurately a destitute – is stretched out on the pathway with a begging bowl by his side. His two feet and one hand are bandaged in old dressings which offer some comfort to the supperating stumps. Yet not one summons an ambulance, or even thinks that they should. He has literally thrown himself at the mercy of the crowds who pass him by. And as you carefully watch the unflinching crowd you will see obviously poor people reaching into their pockets to drop a coin into his bowl as they continue walking without even slowing their pace. It is the reason India has not ground to a halt – the deadly 19th century code of each for himself is tempered by the poor feeling empathy with the great army of those who have fallen by the roadside. Most are only a few stages removed from this situation themselves, and there is a sense of community that cannot be produced by any professional social workers. The Christian relief agencies pick at the problem. But at a Mother Theresa home in Madras the priest calls a meeting to discuss whether a destitute he has been observing on the streets for some days can be spared the one free bed in the home so he can die in peace. Such is the power that any money brings in India. He is brought in, to share the sense of light in this hospice for the dying. A place where a man who has starved for years will eat 20 bowls of rice if they are placed in front of him, he has learnt to eat whenever he can, for the next meal is never certain.

The majority of Indians live on the outside of organised,

A man lies wailing on the footpath with a begging bowl beside him. An everyday sight for the inhabitants of poor Bombay, but if you stand here for a few minutes you will notice the odd good Samaritan dropping a few coins into his bowl.

politically run society. They can only watch from far as new tower blocks arise, TV transmissions beam out in colour, satellites shoot into the Indian skies. The children of the élite are drilled in schools where uniforms, marching and the old British ethic of discipline still reign. They have little knowledge of the old Bombay with its decaying makeshift houses, the night-time streets a patchwork of beds and blankets, where hygiene is hardly known.

By day, the streets of prostitutes around Grant Road look like any other run-down area of the town, the women look after children, do their household chores, groom themselves in preparation for the evening when they will metamorphose into harlots of the night. Now it is the old East of dusty streets, eking out a living, the debris and dirt all around that accompanies early industrialisation. All materials are gathered in streets devoted to a particular trade, in one street corrugated iron sheets, in another glass, further on parts of engines. But the pace is leisurely, for most, with breaks to drink tea, to watch, to listen to itinerant musicians.

If you told these toilers that they had been excluded from the riches of the new world of technology, they would not believe you. For they are at heart the much-spoken-of small entrepreneurs, in some streets they are now taking apart and reassembling complex transistorised machines, learning as they go, showing a ready Eastern flair for the complex and minute.

In the crowded shop that acts as a school, too, you find signs of the coming India. Approximately 50 children sit shoulder to shoulder in the shop. They shout out their tables with a powerful energy which hints at a determination to thrust ahead and ellipse time.

The Indian élite pursue their goal of self-sufficiency, safe in the knowledge that a new army of trained minds is pushing into the great void left by the departure of their former masters.

The decaying bureaucracy the British left behind will next be assaulted and cleansed as the pressure of population growth demands a far greater speed in the central decision making process.

In the Churchgate area, where the banks and airline offices are to be found, the round futuristic tower of the Ambassador Hotel flies the flags of many nations. A country rich in people can look out at the whole world and not feel daunted. For in their own country many races live in a remarkable peace, a microcosm for the whole world to gaze upon and seek to learn from.

A performing monkey posing as a policeman. The Indian police are one of the few unarmed police forces left in the world, though they have been known to shoot rampaging mobs without too many qualms of conscience. It is truly terrifying to see animal instincts take over an Indian mob, they act as one berserk creature.

Chance occurrences

11

In India, guides simply appear. The guides of chance, coincidence or human contact. Whatever is at the back of your mind, whatever brought you to India, will quickly be made manifest. Every meeting, with this realisation, becomes charged with intensity; it is as if only those with some purpose have alighted upon these shores. It may be·true, for though India's treasure houses have been rifled over many centuries, the kernel of wisdom yet remains.

In the holy city of Benares, centre of learning for more than 2,000 years, Europeans now come for short courses in the ancient Hindu learning. These courses run from a minimum of 3 months to 2 years and more. Once accepted, a student has only to find the tiny amount for his rent. There is even an international guest house on the great sprawling campus of the Hindu university for students who have found their way there from all over the world. In Benares are to be found the best teachers of Ayurvedic medicine, Indian music, astrology, Sanskrit. Teachers with a dedication to knowledge, and its transmission to worthy pupils.

I ponder over the chance meeting in a first class railway carriage of just such a student. We are both travelling to Varanasi (a revival of the ancient name for Benares). He is a Colombian who qualified

Previous page Outside the presidential residence in New Delhi, a massive sculpture depicts Ghandi, leading the Indian nation to freedom. Ghandi may have been a shrewd lawyer but as an economist his vision of a self-sufficient rural industry in India has proved to be something of a blind alley. The country has kept alive through rapid industrial growth as the population has surged in numbers.

Stand in front of the destination board at Delhi station and a slow realisation of both the size of the subcontinent and its millions of inhabitants will come to you. Train stations are one of the centres of Indian life and also an easy place to sleep the night if stuck.

in acupuncture in Rumania over a period of 7 years. His yoga teacher there is now disqualified from teaching — since yoga has become one of the 'subversive' arts. The student talks of sophology — a combination of the teachings of Western psychology, Chinese acupuncture and Indian Ayurvedic medicine. It is a new way of treating the body and mind together, two sides of one overall entity. The student tells me of a Nepalese doctor in Goa who has established an ashram to dispense his knowledge. You are forced to think of American medical college professors who earn vast amounts of money, and yet have nothing to pass on. In India, knowledge is still prized for itself, rather than for its commercial use. And who can say that in the West many such professors exist, when promotion depends upon being accepted for publication in a learned journal?

Booking an Indian plane or train at short notice is a hazardous business. I try to book a flight from Bombay to Benares for the next day. No tickets. Eventually the calm desk clerk finds an alternative route. I can fly to New Delhi and then take the train from there. Most Indian Airline flights you quickly discover are fully booked, you need to make reservations days in advance and make sure your booking is confirmed. At the moment, all bookings are confirmed manually, and stories of flights being chronically

The closest shave you will ever get in your life is from an Indian barber. Two complete shaves with a cut-throat razor smoothed over with a sharply stinging balm. At 10 to 15 pence a time, it is far easier and comparable in cost to buying razor blades and then doing the job yourself. India abounds in small physical comforts and comforters.

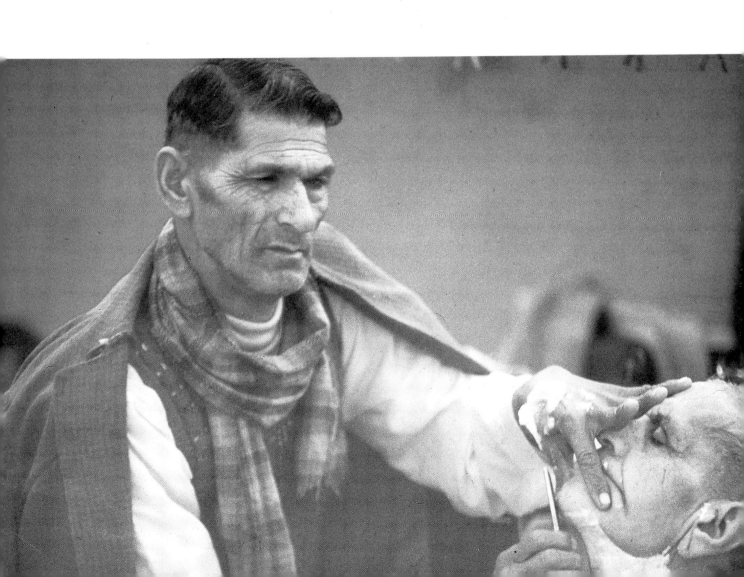

overbooked are factual. Yet the service is cheap by Western standards and, compared with other means of getting around the subcontinent, a plane trip with an hostess who joins her hands together in submissive welcome, is a pleasure or at least a sign of relative freedom from the stress of travel.

At Delhi airport a guide quickly approaches me. He makes his living from taking tourists in his friend's taxi to the Taj Mahal, 150 miles south. But he survives by solving problems. Quickly he finds me the booking office for train tickets. I book the last reserved first-class sleeper to Benares. Two hours later I am on the train. Miraculously, even though the booking office is two miles distance from Delhi station, the carriage has a stenciled list of the names of the passengers, including the author's, stuck outside. Anything complicated, intricate and bureaucratic in nature, finds an Indian response of ingenuity.

Even though the ticket office assured me I was taking the last place, I discover that they have paired me with the only other European on the train. It is either coincidence or the result of planning somewhere by someone. He is from Columbia, and has been studying in India for the last year at Benares University. He has just spent some time with friends in Bombay. We quickly establish a rapport of like interests. What are the origins of Sanskrit, one of the world's most subtle languages which must be studied for 40 years if all the nuances are to be mastered? Every text is written so that it can be read at many levels from the

India has the second largest railway network in the world and approximately half the locomotives are steam driven. For *afficionados* of an era of steam it is a wallowing nostalgia to travel here, but the omnipresent crowds make it an onerous if memorable experience. Booking first class eases the trauma.

Passengers rush a third-class carriage, as they must if they are to have any hope of getting a seat. First class is about 3 or 4 times more expensive than third, but still only approximately £2.50 for 100 miles. The most popular trains on the most popular routes are booked days in advance, but by going on the reserved list and giving generous tips, places do materialise. There is, for example, a special allocation for tourists and VIPs on most trains.

transcendental to the profane. Words denote a certain quality . . . and its opposite. Even though it takes so long to learn completely, there are still Brahmin families in India who use Sanskrit at home (similar to but more complex than the use of Latin by courts and church authorities). It is a language which takes us back to centuries before the birth of Christ, to 1500BC at least when the invaders of India, the Aryans, were also expanding West to colonise Europe. The common roots of words like father and water conclusively point to our origins in the Central Asian vastnesses. The gypsies who spread out from India in the Middle Ages and drifted to Europe by way of Egypt were simply the latecomers following a common migratory pattern.

The rails click by outside. It could almost be England as the great lush sprawling countryside is overtaken by night. In village India the fields are laboriously tilled by oxen and manpower, women carry great loads upon their heads and walk with regal straight backs. Great crops of winter wheat wave in the light gusts of wind. 'The green revolution' has meant that crops can be grown three times a year, and famine has become a memory even though as recently as 1970 it was known. Better breeding, irrigation schemes and sheer tenacity have slowly given the earth its chance to provide for burgeoning numbers. Strangely, the land still looks vast and thinly populated, it is just that wherever you go there are always a few people about.

Kathmandu Valley

12

Flying into the valley of Kathmandu provides a rare opportunity to imprint exactly where you are located upon the mind. Especially when it is possible to take a plane from Benares to Kathmandu for £50 return, and the alternative is a day's winding journey by rail and then another day of travelling up through the Himalayan foothills on very bumpy roads. Kathmandu is located at 4,000 feet above sea level, a valley in the Himalayas, so that in the summer time it is a welcome relief from the scorching plains with temperatures around 90°F instead of 110°F, while in autumn and spring it is a delightfully pleasant environment. In the monsoon period the clouds have lost much of their load by the time they have climbed up into the mountains. In winter, it is cold but the sunshine gives immediate warmth when, as is usual, the skies are clear.

In the crystal clear air the vast chain of white-capped Himalayan peaks can be seen on three sides of the valley, looking even closer than their 20 or 30 miles and very obviously forming the leading edge of what is a continent-sized island of mountains that includes all the 15,000 feet plateau of Tibet, that begins in Afghanistan and stretches 1500 miles to Burma, that is still uncharted territory in many areas. Scale such as this is found nowhere else on earth.

The kingdom of Nepal first opened its borders to 'foreigners' 30 years ago. Much has changed in that time, but even more has stayed the same. Walk through the paddy fields outside the town of Kathmandu at night and in the moonlight that turns everything a rich satisfying blue the pagoda shapes of the temples instantly tell you of the Chinese influence that reigned supreme in Nepal until the 19th century. You are in the China you immediately know from willow patterned chinaware, yet it is only in Nepal that these idyllic peaceful scenes have remained undisturbed. Across the border, no more than 60 miles away, economic plans carried out with a thorough going alacrity have left little of the Middle Kingdom's past extant. Visit the Chinese embassy here, with crowds of Tibetan women talking to the guards, go up to the border to see the new nation arising there, and you become aware of the vast cauldron of change that is the East today. It is here that the 21st century is being blueprinted for the bulk of the world's population.

But as you wander round the old part of Kathmandu you are presented with a picture of centuries-old wooden houses, with no glass in the windows, ground floors still given over to the animals – cows, goats, chickens – narrow muddy lanes along which small men and women carry great loads with a patient toiling energy. You are back in the Middle Ages, a time of romance, a sense of belonging, a backdrop of sudden disease and death. Unlike the towns of India, you are not the centre of attention. Instead, the people glide quietly past, content to co-exist as the unique Nepalese blend of Hinduism, Buddhism and ancient animistic beliefs teaches.

Nepal, everyone will rightly tell you, is a place to unwind and relax after the sheer intensity of India and its constant stunning of the senses. Women in particular find it a relief to get away from the Hindu prurient interest in white bodies and be among a people who have always accepted an active role for the female. Kathman-

Loaded with bowls, a Nepalese walks through the main market square in the old part of Kathmandu. Here there are many wooden buildings going back centuries. During the rainy season from July to September these picturesque dirt lanes and squares become very muddy but that is part of the charm.

du is immensely seductive, a place of smiling children and Tibetans, a place where there is space to be yourself, it is a society still at the early stages of coming to terms with the 20th century. Even though there is a flourishing and profitable market in Western gadgetry and cars. If you bring along a camera, a watch, a portable stereo, a calculator, you can sell them at prices that will pay for your journey.

However, as always, the real essential Nepal lies outside the capital. The 'twin' towns of Bhatgaon and Patan, also in the 25 mile valley, and former challengers of Kathmandu's dominance, are far quieter places than Kathmandu. While if you go walking or trekking the 90 miles to Pokhra in the shadow of the mighty Annapurna mountains, you will be in some of the most undisturbed and beautiful country in the world, with only the mosquitoes to remind you that you have not entered heaven.

Slowly you become aware of how little the people subsist on. A 'mug-size' bowl of rice and vegetables twice a day. Yet the young women will stride past you on steeply climbing mountain slopes, their bare feet finding places to alight among the sharp rocks with unerring accuracy, their speed leaving you far behind in spite of the heavy load they will almost inevitably be carrying. Mountain people, the world over, have a vigour and matter of factness about them that instantly reveals the affectations of 'civilisation'.

But even though washing in mountain streams, lying down on bare rock to soak in the sun, breathing in the exhilarating air, eating well and heartily, you will not escape for very long the harsh side of this life. Women file past your open window in the narrow lanes wailing the sudden death of a neighbour. There is no Indian philosophical acceptance here. The water supply is polluted, not least from the fields being used as a vast communal lavatory so that the contamination filters through first to the water table and then to the water supplies. The kitchens of the cafès you eat in are dark, dirty and dank. Animals are sacrificed to appease unknown avenging gods. The mountain tribal people sweep into town for joyous celebrations, exhibiting an awesome energy that they must possess to match the extremes of their environment. And yet Kathmandu is always a very hard place to leave. Here you come face to face with yourself and find it not an unpleasant experience.

A typical shop in the old part of town. Nepal has an even lower standard of living than India. But it has also become a traditional trading post for the sale of Western gadgetry – cameras, watches, transistor radios and cassette players are all eagerly snapped up at good prices.

The holy city of Benares

13

The old *sadhu* – perhaps 70, perhaps much more – is clothed in orange and yellow robes, while upon his head is a turban of similar colours and his brow is covered in brilliant ochre coloured dyes. He is carried along on a raised chair by celebrating men to the joyful accompaniment of drums and symbols. You hear the music before they appear in the narrow lane and are immediately drawn to the inert figure of the man, whose whole body jerks with every movement of those who carry his triumphal chair upon their shoulders. Death must be very near, and yet there is a mood of a wedding procession. To the Hindus, death in Benares is the most propitious of all, it means that the cycle of coming and going has come to an end, and that the soul can go to become part of the universal. It is the end of a journey that began many thousands of years ago.

The procession's destination is the waterside where bodies are burnt on great piles of wood. Ships loaded with the logs are moored just by the great slabs of stone which rise up in steps from the river. These *ghats* have remained unchanged for many hundreds of years. Smoke rises from the fires that take three hours to burn a body. The conical shapes of temples penetrate the mist-like smoke while birds wheel incessantly above the scene of quiet dignity, and relatives gather to watch the fires burn. Another body clothed in a brightly coloured sheet is placed by the waterside on a stretcher. The funeral assistants splash water upon the corpse's face several times as they make their ritual ablutions. There is no air of grief, only of the correct procedures being followed.

It is utterly unlike the breaking of morning across the great stretch of the Ganges river here, more than half a mile separates one bank from the other even in winter, during the monsoon it can swell to three times that extent. The sun rises slowly from behind the flat plains of Uttar Pradesh. By the *ghats* any unusual quality of light can take you through a time gap to reveal the several thousand-year-old continuous history of this sacred place. Now it is winter, and the light is misty, blue, ghostly, quickly dispersed by the warming sun. The lines of beggars have already taken up their position on the main *ghat* steps leading from the market to the water's edge.

But come in May and the temperature will have soared to past 120°F. Still you will find pilgrims who have travelled here from all over India performing their ritual morning wash in the sacred waters of the Ganges. In the fierce heat, this ceremony, which has been performed so often, with so many prayers offered, takes on a different dimension as bodies shimmer and the huge stone steps float: you are back 3,000 years in time, with the people seeming to glide before you, moving in a slow purposeful way which owes nothing to modern stress. The act of washing is seen as the act of renewal that it is.

There are constant festivals in Benares, always flags flying, music being beat out upon drums and bells, crowds coming to the waterside and then setting out in boats to cast bouquets of flowers upon the waters. Today and tomorrow it is the feast of Saraswati – goddess of learning, the arts, music. Students arrive with great effigies of her, bedecked in flowers, at the waterside. Some of them dancing themselves into a trance, but only the young men

Previous page The great chain of the Himalayas seen from Nagarkot, some 20 miles outside Kathmandu town. The physical presence of the mountains – and the rumblings of far-off gigantic storms – dominates the lives of everyone in Kathmandu Valley. There is a unique atmosphere here that cannot be nailed down yet which pervades everything.

Opposite A man greets the rising sun as it emerges from beyond the plains of Uttar Pradesh on the far side of the river. Every organised tour takes visitors to see the riverside at dawn, where a reverence for the beginning of another day is palpably in the air.

Sacred cows wander the lanes that begin at the top of the bathing *ghats* in Benares, or Varanasi as the government has renamed the town. The temples here look out across the broad Ganges river and have often been built by the Indian *maharajahs*. Although it is impossible to say exactly when the first temples were constructed, the aura of Benares says thousands of years.

are present. The Indian women make a more individual and discreet acknowledgement of their faith.

The great former (and present) houses of the Maharajahs rise up above the *ghats* to four and five stories, presenting an imposing view for those cruising along the river in large rowing boats. (Every tour will take you to see the riverside as it stirs at dawn). Behind these great buildings, the ancient twisting lanes, with their crumbling buildings, their numerous sacred cows and their small wayside shrines, are to be found. It is the heart of the ancient town, where nothing much has changed, the alleyways still follow their former incomprehensible routes.

As dusk comes down, as so often happens, the past becomes alive again. Particularly when the electricity fails, a not infrequent occurrence in India. Lost and stumbling through these alleyways, you sense the people's reluctance to venture far. A reluctance that marked all our predecessors right through almost to modern times. It is only now that the world's people are beginning to lay claim to their planet instead of one small part. Only now that they are seeing what has been done in their name by rulers operating at a distance. Once the damage is realised, then will come the urge to work in harmony once again with the earth.

The river is now absolutely quiet. It is night. A few lights pick out already swathed figures who will sleep out in the surprising chill of the Indian winter here when temperatures drop to the mid-40s. The distant barking of dogs carries clearly across the still water. India retires early, and you quickly fall into the same rhythm. A drum briefly breaks into the silence, then a temple bell, then the languor of the night is upon you again. It is the silence we all once knew. Benares is a last fortress against disharmony. Behind the pantheon of gods and goddesses, lies a worship of Shiva and Shakti, the male and female regenerative forces. India has preserved from its long past a respect for our own creative powers, a belief in their consecrating effect. Where we seek to subdue, the Hindu seeks to be at one with the natural forces. It is a recipe for the ease of tension that the West has induced in itself by a denial of our deepest drives, believing them to be base. Hinduism would disagree.

Previous page Devoid of the grey bleakness of Western funerals, relatives quietly watch as a dead person is consumed in the flames of a funeral pyre. There is a dense air of mysteriousness in the vicinity of the burning *ghats*, and it is one of the few Hindu holy places banned to photographers.

Witnessing the creation

14

The early morning mist slowly disperses under the influence of the warming sun at the *ghats*. A bespectacled *sadhu* with grey long hair is tidying away his few belongings into a small bundle. He looks, and is, perfectly content. He inspires an utter respect for the creation which announces itself so dramatically here each day, which is supercharged with the witness of so many saintly figures through the centuries. And in spite of the increasing bustle to be found upon the Indian streets, it is still possible here in Benares to find a direct continuation of the old line of Indian philosophy.

It is a philosophy that finds its intertwining some 2,500 years ago. Then the native Indian respect for life and its creative forces, for the spirits of the trees, plants, rocks, all of the creation, came into contact with the highly evolved philosophy of the Aryans, who lived in the central Asian steppes probably near the Caspian Sea. Our own ancestors moved west century by century into

The cast of dawn upon the horizon, two children set out with their loads of flowers to sell to pilgrims. The offerings are floated upon the sacred Ganges waters, with a lighted taper set among the flowers, to slowly drift downstream in the direction of the distant Bay of Bengal.

Europe, displacing the aboriginal inhabitants who appear in Britain, at least, to have been short dark people who can still be found in Wales, Scotland and Ireland. Some of these Aryan peoples, speaking various dialects of the Sanskrit mother language – hence the Indo-European group of languages – moved south and east to India. They drank an hallucinatory drug called *soma* and had space in the endless steppes to have spent much time pondering the nature of existence.

These same conclusions can be read both in the ancient Upanishads and Vedas and in the modern interpretations of latter-day Indian saints, a line that can be traced back to Ramakrishna Parmahansa who taught in late 19th century Calcutta. His disciples include Swami Vivekananda, Sri Aurobindo and Yogananda of 'Autobiography of a Yogi' fame. The Divine Life Society with an ashram in Rishikesh also stems from this root. The philosophy is based upon the continuing evolution of man's consciousness being fed back to the planet as it proceeds upon its evolution to a higher state.

Opposite The backlanes of Benares contain a multitude of shrines. This lingam is already decorated with flowers, striking confirmation of how the sophistication of Hindu philosophy has been married to the simple yet potent practices of an earlier animistic fertility-worshipping religion. All India still reverberates with the mysteries, dark inner rooms, the old light of understanding gained from *soma* – an ancient Aryan hallucinogenic.

The temple of Shakti, high above the Ganges. It is early in the morning, the gates of dawn and those of the temple are opened at approximately the same time by priests. Their dignity echoes long centuries of hallowed practice.

But all this sounds entirely theoretical until you meet an exponent of its teachings. The yoga of action (karma) in the world depends upon knowledge (jnana) and this leads to devotion (bhakti yoga). In the sadhu's eyes is awe and worship of the creation in front of his eyes. He declines to be photographed and makes you realise the trifling nature of such an interruption. He says not a word, but gives off a feeling of beatitude as he surveys the beginning of another blessed day, as they all have been, for those that have eyes to see.

Past the sadhu, at the top of the steep ghats is a tiny temple where within its quadrangle nandi bulls – dedicated to Shiva – are sculpted in white marble. Another echo back to the time when the bull was universally a sacred fertility symbol, some 4,000 years ago.

A priest has come into the temple quadrangle. An angular man of about 45 who proceeds with the morning ritual. He sings 'Om Shiva' in front of the locked gates of the central shrine within the quadrangle, rattles the gates, inside is huge lingam bedecked with flowers. He then sprinkles water on the tiny lingam and yoni shrines set into the walls of the quadrangle. At one corner is a second shrine dedicated to Shakti, Shiva's consort. Here the priest is joined by other priests – red and orange marked upon their third eye between and slightly above the eyebrows. They look out across the brilliant Ganges river below. It is re-entering the Greek and Roman era of reverence for the mysteries. And Benares is at least this old.

Away from the temple in the twisting lanes, the houses also have interior quadrangles just as in ancient Roman houses. These lanes can both delight and shock. One minute you are looking at a wagging tailed pup, the next the severed head of a more unfortunate pup. Children quietly smile as you pass, the morning has a wonderful peace. Then you emerge from the back lanes into the hubbub of the modern India where motorised rickshaws, scooters, bicycles and cars jostle with crowds of people for space.

The wealth of Benares – eternal city of pilgrimage – is displayed in the tiny shops of the back streets. Beautifully woven shawls of pure merino wool, brightly coloured bracelets, richly smelling perfumes, copperware, jewellery of every fantastic shape, brocades glinting and shining in the sunlight and later the flickering light of hurricane lamps. A purchase can be made leisurely over a cup of chai, seated upon cushions, there is always time here.

As night descends on the main streets, an incredible traffic jam of people, cars, bikes and scooters develops. But no-one loses their temper when a car does a U-turn and brings the driftwood of people to a sluggish halt.

Back at the river, and the houseboats which can be hired for a pound a day, there is still the old quiet. Incense wafting from the temples, late night drinkers of tea gathered around a warming stove. On return to the houseboat two cats jump off its roof, reach the shore and safety by leaping from rowing boat to rowing boat. Through the open window of the houseboat the sound of the river gently lapping against the hull, all is silence and wonder again. A spell.

Celebration, consultation, education

15

There is a certain magnificence about New Delhi. Mostly conveyed by the wide avenues which lead to government buildings designed in the 1930s as Britain clung on to the 'jewel of the Empire'. You will have seen these avenues in the film Gandhi (Oscar-winning it may have been, but it did not dwell too long on the rather odd private man). More difficult to appreciate from a film is the way that India sends a kaleidoscope of sights and sensations all through any day. In the capital it is a procession of camel riders rehearsing for the celebration of the Republic's birthday, all in brightly decked uniforms. This is followed by a wedding party, with the women wearing their most creatively swirling-coloured sarees, with a gold figured man upon a horse decked in silver, led by a New Orleans style jazz band.

But it is at Benares that the Indian style of celebration finds its most pure and authentic expression. Brightly coloured garlands of magnificently scented and profusely prodigal flowers, the insistent ever-changing patterns of tabla beats, finely tuned bells ringing out at all times of the day and night, even above the cacophony of dogs at night rivalling other packs further down the river in the fierceness of their cries.

Working from tattered Sanskrit texts kept in linen wrappings, the astrologer makes his calculations while a visiting palmist examines the client's hand. Weddings and other important events are determined with the help of the astrologer's advice. Often uncannily accurate.

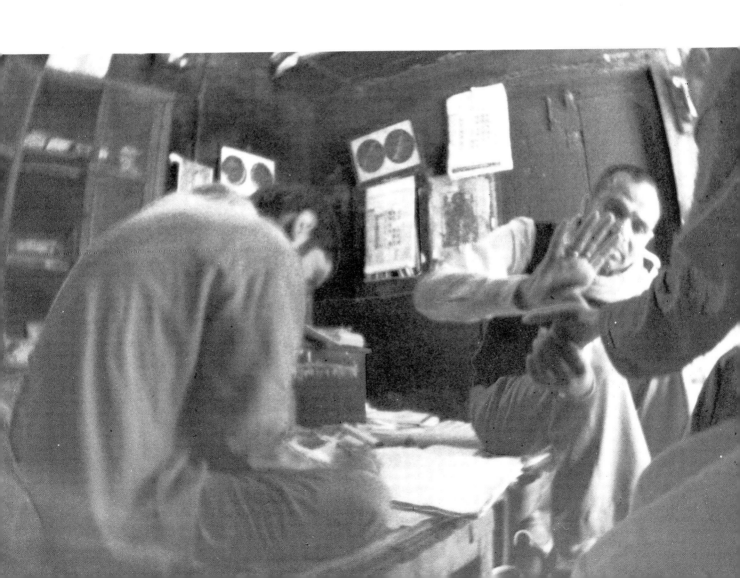

In the vegetable market by the *ghats* is the heart of India. Freshly grown produce laid out upon leaves to be inspected by the passing pilgrims and townspeople. From dawn until well past dusk, the strongly coloured sarees of the peasant women provide a splash of gaiety to the more subtle colours of their piles of peas and potatoes, grapes and oranges. The streets of India are alive with human bustle – no other country can match both the sheer intensity and variety of street life – where most still ply their trade, and many have no other home. Ten in the evening and you find the vegetable sellers wrapped up in shawls, huddled in groups by the roadside, ready for another night, still rustling with animation as a surge of life passes through the group. Tribal living.

Early in the day the beggars – some *sadhus*, more cripples and lepers – begin their daily importuning of the passers by with as much energy as any other trader. If these unfortunate people were to be caught in some safety net provided by the government, then the street traders and peasant women would wonder why they had to spend all day selling their produce to earn some five or ten rupees (30 pence or 60 pence). The Indian economy will need to become far wealthier, efficient and corruption free before it can break out of the cycle of subsistence living. And yet, here it has always been so. The records of the East India Company speak of appalling poverty and famines. At least now there is little obvious starvation to be seen, there are far fewer lepers than 15 years ago as the wonders of antibiotics work their magic. And it is on this painful scale of misery that the country's progress can be easily measured.

India's learned citizens live little higher above the subsistence level themselves. The astrologer who has been schooled in the ancient learning by his astrologer father spends three hours for a consultation that costs 180 rupees – £12. He unties bundles of Sanskrit texts from their linen covers. His relatives and fellow astrologers come to see him as he makes, from their point of view, his astonishingly well-paid calculations. Indian astrology differs from Western astrology significantly, yet the predictions the astrologer makes accord with what a Western astrologer would deduce. He asks the German girl if France is near Germany, tells her that she will marry a farmer and live in France. She is studying agriculture, and this is certainly what she would like to do.

One of the astrologer's students is a very prescient 14-year-old called Gobin. He is the son of a temple priest who now lives in Madras. Being a Brahmin, Gobin knows that his future lies in mastering the ancient learning. He already speaks better English than his teacher, and is more familiar with Western gadgetry. After a few minutes he has mastered the functions of the latest Pentax camera, and indeed owns a camera himself. Gobin looks, and is, entirely sure of himself. He does not smoke or drink because it is 'injurious to health'. He is here to learn, that he knows and proceeds accordingly. And this is how the ancient Indian knowledge is passed on, on a master-pupil basis, just as it was in Europe in the Middle Ages.

Shri L.R. Nayak has learnt the enormous subtleties of the sitar over many years – and when an instrument harks back to the very beginning of music in its deeply vibrant sounds, then the mastering of all its possibilities takes time. He runs an international music school where students can come for periods of study. A month,

Previous page At the first hints of dawn, Benares stirs. Already pilgrims will be ritually washing themselves for renewal and freedom from past wrongs. The fruit market will soon be open, and the delicious *curd* – yogurt – will be ready. In India it is a crime not to be up early.

In a stonemason's workshop, the figure of George V stands in magnificent disregard among Indian busts. The days of the Raj, with its seeming orderliness, are looked back to fondly by some of the older Indians. However, the bulk of the population was born after Independence in 1947.

An appreciation of the sitar's vast range of sound comes from hearing the instrument in the hands of a master. Formerly with Indian radio, L R Nayak runs an 'international music school' in the very oldest cramped part of Benares. About 20 people study there at any one time, from all over the Western world.

three months or the full 7 years it takes to become a master. His son is a tabla player who also spends much of his day teaching in the traditional one-to-one manner. Now Western students, disillusioned with the anonymity of vast lecture theatres in their universities are finding their way to this old centre of learning. Students are accepted at Benares university for either short or long periods. It is not hard to predict that India will become one of the world centres of learning in the 21st century.

The address of the music school is D 33/81 Khalishpura Varanasi. The astrologer is: Deo ni Nanclan Shastri, GK 3516, Saraswati Phatak, Varanasi–221001. (Near Golden Temple).

A severed head

16

While the Vedic religion of India can be traced back with some certitude to 2,500 years ago, the religions it incorporated are lost in a far more distant time. Yet, at Benares you sense many reminders of the antiquity of this earlier line. You see a naked man carrying a staff, a *sadhu* devoted to a worship of nature. The breadth of the river, which swells to nearly two miles across at monsoon time and can climb up the mighty stone blocks of the *ghats* to the maharajah's palatial homes at the steps' top, is a fitting environment to contemplate simplicity and the power of the earth. The sunrise seen from the *ghats* takes place over flat sweeping countryside that harks back to the time when the Indian subcontinent detached itself from Africa, Australia and Antartica and began its 'rapid' journey across the equator to collide with the Asian landmass. The very profuseness of life and plant forms is altogether different from the dry Asian interior, with its barren mountains and the constant battle for survival. Here life thrives in a climate of prolificness, anything can happen, and usually does, but it is at temperatures that are more familiar to the human body than the cold North.

Having been the supporter of life for so long, having changed relatively little, the subcontinent has been able to support continuity, both in the uniqueness and diversity of its animal and plant life, also in the lingering appreciation of the mothering earth.

Energy, power, the wisdom of intuitive knowledge. A tantric yoga follower sought these attribtes upon the *ghats* – above the burning pyres of precious wood which a Hindu must save religiously for during his life if he is going to be able to afford his burial according to the ancient rites. Finally, he found this growth and wisdom from becoming a devotee of Shakti, symbol of female sexual energy. The whole of Benares is dedicated to Shiva, her male counterhalf, so that is not surprising. You have only to see the loincloth clad *sadhus* carrying the triple pointed rod of Shiva, crowned with three orange flowers, to realise the incredibly remote ancestry of this form of worship. And of tantric yoga – which says that a disciple must follow his desires through to their conclusion, to master the power they have over him and which he can then use.

There is one enigmatic symbol of this man's discovery of power to heal, to expand, to nurture. A head set in the upper storey of a house in a small niche.

The follower of Shakti found the head in the ruins of an ancient Benares house. Now, 14 years after he died, the head lives on, gazing out over a narrow alleyway in the oldest part of the town, just behind the *ghats*. The lines of the head are clear cut and symmetrical. It could be an Egyptian or Roman head. Certainly it speaks of that time in recorded antiquity when Greece flourished, and China. A time when there were less questions, more certitudes. The rate of change has disturbed our modern sense of the vast supporting body of the world which does not change. The head is living history, reminder of undreamt powers, now almost forgotten and liable to be buried in the rubble left by the march of modernisation. To the Indians Benares is a very backward place, but then places of religious pilgrimage often are.

You note in the townspeople an accumulated, unconscious

Opposite Mysteriously beautiful, calm and powerful – a head of the goddess Shakti. Found in a ruined building by a devotee who spent years penetrating her secrets while meditating upon the burning *ghats*. There are definite links with the ancient world of Egypt in this stunning face.

A celebration in honour of the goddess Saraswati – patron of the arts, music and students. It is the young men who work themselves into a frenzy as they follow the effigy to the banks of the Ganges accompanied by the beat of drums. The young girls watch from a distance, equally fervent in their own way.

civilisation. There is in Baluchistan, a province of Pakistan next to Afghanistan, a similar town called Quetta. Archaeologists have now had to revise their calculations of how long ago it was that Quetta first had an advanced city structure, with traders and craftsmen, planned streets and sanitation. Their present answer is 5,000 years. If you watch the tall elegant tribesmen smoking their water pipes in fuggy back rooms, you travel back to this time, and note the incredible grace of the people, their manual dexterity, their sureness, in a word their civilisation.

Benares' inhabitants also have this anceent lineage indelibly stamped upon them. You meet masseurs who know every part of the body and can expertly clear any blockage. The children fly their kites with an uncanny ability that has been passed from child to child in the backstreets for thousands of years.

Night time is the best opportunity to sense this still living past. In the lanes that wind inexplicably from the burning *ghats* there are hardly any lights, muffled figures pass you, dogs growl, occasional gleams from tiny shops cast some illumination for your faltering steps, temples seem to be dotted all around, you are in a reverential world which has not yet committed the sin of hubris.

At the same time that you are in a different state of mind, you are also unmistakably in the present. You lose your conditioning, your baggage, there is nothing tugging you away, the past has slipped, your past, and the future will come, while in the present is peace, calm and respect for what we are given.

And once you sense what it is like to be fully alive, you are no longer seeking answers, it is as though once you are able to formulate a question, then the answer too must be known. The aura of Benares, fabricated by millions of the devout over thousands of years, is irresistible. It is a glimpse into the laws of life.

In a serenely peaceful back lane in Benares, a pup surveys the early morning, vigorously alive and blissfully unaware of the struggle for survival that all the young in India must contend with. Many are casualties along the way, but the Hindu respect for life ensures that all have their chance.

Village India

17

A statistical description of India is as richly confusing as any visual impression. An average income per head of 750 rupees a year (£50). This income has grown by only 50% since independence day on August 15, 1947. Yet inflation has decreased the purchasing power of the rupee by several hundred per cent. At the same time India has become one of the 10 leading industrial producers in the world.

Population growth goes some way to explaining this contradiction. For the numbers of Indians have almost doubled to over 700 millions since 1947. More statistics: the landmass is half that of Europe, within its confines you will find 14 major languages, so that the 'national' language is spoken by less than half the population and in the South there are very few who speak it. The literacy rate is around 35%. English is spoken by 10% of the population, generally the ruling élite. Jobs for the highly qualified, such as sales engineers with degrees and five or six years experience, are rewarded with pay of just over £100 a month. There is a growing unemployment problem, growing inflation, yet economic growth has only recently slowed from a healthy 8% p.a. A better rate than that of even Japan.

Slowly threading their way into the town of Pushkar from their village across the desert, these Rajasthani men pass a solitary temple beside a deep well. Behind their easy-going manner is a steel determination, for these are the inheritors of the Rajput warrior code which enjoins a fight to the death.

The reality behind this shimmering patchwork of statistics is that the great bulk of the Indian population live on the very fringes of the cash economy. Their homes are ochre-coloured mud-walled houses in the villages. Their labour is in the fields behind oxen pulling ploughs, and yet they are the most efficient farmers who produce enough for themselves and some excess to sell in the market. Thanks to the 'green revolution' and the liberal use of fertilisers India has so far kept ahead of its population growth. There are even economists here who talk of India's vast manpower resources, something that the old pioneering 'Peace Corps' women, trying with unremarkable success to promote birth control to the women, would find hard to comprehend. However, for the last 4 years, because of two partial failures of the monsoons, India's grain and pulse production has remained near stationary, having increased by nearly 50% from 1967.

While an educated élite produce more scientific papers than any other 'developing' country, particularly in the areas of physics and chemistry, the great bulk of the population continue to live as they have always done.

Life in the villages is slow. Routine is all. The children wear tattered clothes. And the weather remains the supreme arbiter of destiny. Harvest time is the one time of plenty. But then it was in Europe until the advent of the industrial revolution.

For India to earn the currency that will pay for its low level of imports – oil in particular being an exception to self sufficiency – the produce from the countryside is increasingly exported. Many in the villages are under nourished, but they and their villages will survive any man-made economic disaster as they have done for some 10,000 years. For the villagers' children it is possible that life will change. In theory they get free education to the age of 9 or 10. But the caste system and its consequent lack of opportunity for the rural poor is still remarkably all-pervasive.

A group of Harijans – untouchables – camp out on a dusty patch of ground outside a village. Buffalo, pigs, camels wander about. The Harijans have been here for 5 years, about as welcome as a gypsy encampment in Bromley. Cow dung dries in the sun, there is no feeling of purpose or activity, in its place an almost meditational presence. A young Harijan girl drives some pigs towards the distant outline of a temple *stupa* upon the hill. In front of the eternal Hindu verities she is equal, but the social structure insists that she is outside caste society which is divided and subdivided into thousands of categories. The *Brahmin* class provide the scholars and holymen, the priests and teachers, the *Kshatriyas* the warriors and princes, the *Vaishyas* the merchants and traders, the *Sudras* the artisans. Most castes have little to do with one another, it has been the Indian way of combining utterly different races, religions and philosophies together.

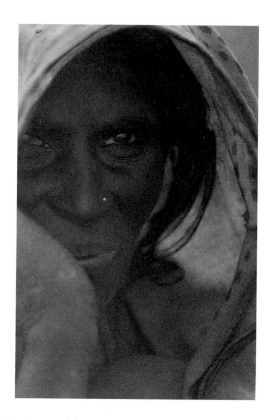

A woman who helps at an Indian cafe sits down in the heat of the day and observes the slowly-moving scene around her. The intense concentration upon the present is etched into her impassive face.

So is the Harijan girl happy or unhappy as she drives her pigs? It is not the right question. Her attitude is unquestioning, she is removed from a sense of progress or even time. The day begins, moves to a climax, comes to its end. To survive poverty you do not ask how you will survive tomorrow. Attending to the matters of the day demands attention enough. And are not most of the West's ills derived from a chronic fear of the future? Fear of the loss of what one has. Fear of unannounced disaster. It is as if the Westerner fears retribution, as if he feels he does not deserve what he has and so must defend it with unreasonable vehemence.

Village India supports the whole crazy Indian excess of bureaucratic regulation, official corruption, cynicism and world weariness. A small self-perpetuating entity — the ruling élite — is fed by the silent millions toiling in the fields.

The rivers of India have been her highways from earliest history. There are records of trade with China and the Roman Empire, but it was Chinese sailors who carried the wares. Invaders have usually followed the routes of the Ganges and its tributaries since the time of the Greek invasion under Alexander the Great.

Pushkar lake

18

Above the holy lake of Pushkar, Rajasthan, stands a steeply climbing mountain at the top of which is a temple outlined against the pink of a sunset sky. In the valley where the lake is found, surrounded by the vigorously rising mountains with the desert beyond, there are over 50 temples. They all surround the placid waters of a great lake, which has been a centre of Hindu worship for at the least some thousands of years. The whole of Pushkar is dedicated to Brahma, the creator in the Hindu trinity, and it is therefore a very holy place. Anyone who visits here is immediately captivated by the integrity of its worship and lifestyle. For the town is sufficiently off the beaten track to have almost wholly resisted both the inflation besetting the industrialised towns and the loss of faith. The nearest railway stop is Ajmer, itself a very old city that figures in Rajasthan's history more than a thousand years ago. A time when invading Arab warriors started a titanic duel with the Rajput warriors as they sought to impose Islamic religion on these people who had come down from central Asia more than 2000 years before.

In spite of many victories, and a warrior code that believes that to die in battle is a supreme glory, Rajasthan was eventually conquered by the Mughal invaders in the 16th century but Rajasthan always kept its own culture, and traditions. It does so today to a remarkable extent. The men wear extremely long and brilliantly coloured turbans, which can be unwound to form a protection against sudden dust storms.

The reverence for tradition finds its outward signs in the way that all these 50 temples have attendant priests who cater for the needs of the constantly arriving pilgrims from all over India. Many seem prosperous by Indian standards and there are several hundred priests who exist on the offerings of these pilgrims. Showers of Indian coins surround an underground shrine to Shiva — a garlanded lingam and yoni. The temple is brilliantly painted in soft pinks and blues and greens, while it is crowned with a bulbous minaret, silent testimony to the strong Persian influence in this North Western corner of India, next to the Pakistan border. Many of the temples show the same ornateness in design that can be found in the mosques of Iran, Afghanistan and Pakistan. And it was this Rajasthan combination of influences that gave rise to the Raj's perpetuation of the style in the imperial governmental buildings of New Delhi.

The Rajput warriors' defence of their romantic homeland, with its sweep of deserts and craggy hilltops and mountains, is understandable once you experience the quiet beauty of Pushkar lake. It is a place to value and if necessary to die for. And when defeat came, the Rajput women would throw themselves upon fires rather than live in abject servitude. The mass immolation of *jauhor* is recorded on at least three occasions.

With so many pilgrims, there is a sizeable population of *sadhus* to be found at the approaches to the temples. At the main temple, there are tiny 'cells' set into the walls just outside the gates. Here the Hindu pilgrims come up to a *sadhu* who is sitting placidly on a flat raised terrace outside his cell. They change their rupee notes into paisa coins with the sadhu who has very Tibetan features, slightly slanting eyes, a reddish brown skin and high cheekbones.

An aquiline face gazes out from a passing train. You speculate on the the man's heritage. Before the British, the Mughals were supreme, before them Mongol warriors including the terrible Tamerlaine. Is this the face of a descendant of the Mongol hordes who wreaked such terrible deprivation? In India, as in most of Eurasia, folk memory lingers of that most deadly of times.

He obliges them without losing the quiet calm intensity of his consciousness. It sounds like a very intellectual cool achievement but you realise, studying the open countenance, it is almost a childlike awareness and interest in the world about him, unclouded by extraneous dark thoughts. Next to him on the terrace, a girl of 6 or 7 collects a few more coins from the passing pilgrims and hands them over to him. Another Indian pilgrim, dressed in shirt and slacks asks for a 5 rupee note to be changed into singles. He is obviously pleased and impressed to have dealings with the *sadhu*, (many Indians can recognise saintliness in their midst). Yet he also queries the condition of one of the notes he receives. (Indians are afraid of having old paper money rejected, and therefore prefer to stay in a coin economy; the more remote the region, the greater the likelihood of having tattered notes rejected by nervous shopkeepers).

After some time sitting with the *sadhu* on the terrace outside the gates of the temple, you become aware that one arm is not visible, and that it probably ends in a stump within the folds of the orange robe he is wearing. However, this man's face shines with a light and life that has overcome his disability, or rather the body's disability and vagary, he laughs it off. Beside him, outside the next tiny cell, similarly decorated with the ubiquitous popular calendar

With a radiant glow upon his clear face, this saffron clad *sadhu* sits outside his cell at the entrance to the main temple in Pushkar. The infallible test of any holy man – how the children treat him – is perfectly illustrated by the eagerness with which the children help him change the money of tourists into small coins for offerings inside the temple.

An 'untouchable' outside the gates of a temple. Behind him is a young Brahmin – the priestly caste. The Indians have difficulty slotting Europeans into the all-pervasive caste system, so they all feel free to talk to visitors, but the young Brahmin will ignore the pipe-player.

Previous page Sunset at Pushkar lake. Fifty temples surround its cold clear waters in a remote desert area of Rajasthan. It is reputed to have been a place of worship for thousands of years and possesses the one temple in India dedicated to Brahma, the creator.

Opposite The only sound to be heard at the lakeside hotel is the sound of pigeons cooing, the gentle chatter of children, the bells of the temples ringing out across the waters. Pushkar is one of those places in India where people go to wind down after the intensity of much of the Indian experience.

illustrations of Hindu gods and goddesses, sits a woman *sadhu* clothed in the saffron colours of one who has chosen the way of renunciation in order to find salvation. Your eyes are immediately attracted by the shining, accepting smile on her face, and it takes some time again to notice that her foot is twisted up, and has only two toes. She does not mind this being noticed and like the man beside her, laughs it off as inconsequential.

The red sun sinks below the horizon as geese and ducks dot the lake. Great lazy fish swim among the luxuriant plants in the cold clear water of the oasis in the desert. A loudspeaker from one of the temples broadcasts the triumphant notes of an Indian trumpet. But it in no way disrupts the pigeons from their cooing on ledges at the tourist hotels gathered on the lake's side, one a former palace, one a former ashram. The lake is quiet enough for the chirps of passing birds to be distinctly heard. Children a hundred yards away at the waterside can be heard chattering excitedly as the day comes to an end.

The simple pleasures

19

Today is the day set aside each year for the celebrations in honour of the carpenters' saint. A jazz band in natty red uniforms precedes a flower-decked figure while the attendant priest lights a flaming torch. It is a reminder that Europe, too, was once like this, in fact it still is in the intricate ritual of the Roman church. In Pushkar, each day is set aside for some celebration so that whatever calling a man has, one day will be especially his. It is a human marking out of the flow of time, a satisfying circular return in the alleged grand scheme of things. Indeed, the Hindu sages have marked out great cycles of time, where 'the time taken for an eagle's feather to wear down a mountain is but the flicker of an eyelid.'

Religious intensity has entirely deserted Europe, still wondering how the constant wars and cold mechanised deaths of the 20th century, could be contained within a Christian framework. In India, this intensity is still alive. It is all too easy for a Westerner to concentrate upon the unfortunate who have been laid low by poverty and disease, but this is the lot of a minority, and it is not the ordinary Indian's life. A film is being run in the covered area between two blocks of houses, forming an instant outside picture palace, nearly half the town comes to watch as soon as night falls, and stays till midnight, eyes never leaving the picture upon the makeshift screen. It is a saga of Mother India. The harvest grows high, men sing happily as they scythe the corn. Pretty smiling girls carry the crop away upon their heads, they are adorned in brilliantly coloured sarees. Escapist the film certainly is, but it is rooted in the hopes and aspirations of the great majority of the country's people.

The majority live in an entirely agrarian society, surrounded by the sights, sounds and smells of animals and plants. A successful harvest is the time of great celebration and rare plenty. Music does come easily to these simple people. They have yet to experience any of the alienation which has crept upon modern man. So the hard won pleasures do delight, and the fecund soil is regarded as blessed. The daily prayer to the *lingam* and *yoni* is for fertility. The rhythm of life, its hazards, its rewards, all these are uppermost in the Indian mind. Faraway in the cities, they envision, there is a more sophisticated eating, drinking, singing and dancing lifestyle. That is the future they would like, and which is played back to them on film. But for now, they accept, it is entirely out of reach.

In a life dependent upon the earth, a faith can easily grow – and a sense of humility when confronted with what is greater. Not for rural India is there yet the hubris of a civilisation which has learnt how to control nuclear forces, and yet cannot control itself. Nor yet is there knowledge of the sterility that can be brought to the land at the touch of a button. Yet the élite of India have created an atom bomb (it is said that an 'exchange' student to Holland decamped with the knowledge) and India has joined that still mercifully small group of nations who possess the power to wreak a terrible new order.

A country or a people or a civilisation that does not worship life, worships death, if only by default. To be removed from the frontline of a divided Europe where rockets carrying nuclear warheads are targeted upon all the major cities by Russians, French, British and Americans, is to become aware of the

Previous page A temple on a mountain looks down on Pushkar lake. Beyond stretches the desert towards the border with Pakistan. In the barren wastes of the Thar, India's first atomic bomb was exploded in 1974. An event discussed by the village people with some awe, for word quickly travelled of a dust cloud that blotted out the sun for three days.

Beside the holy lake of Pushkar are found many pigeons which begin their cooing as the day begins and continue to preen themselves and flutter about among their fellows all day long. In Pushkar nothing disturbs their canoodling.

The goddess Saraswati, bedecked with flowers. In Pushkar there is a celebration of some god or goddess every day. It is a way of dividing up the passing seasons into a measure of time, with a special day set aside for every manner of trade and its patron deity.

production lines still continuing to multiply the killing power of governments. Behind the platitudes of the rivals, and the despair of the unilateralists, it becomes obvious that all are locked into the same deadly vision. It is a fear for the future based upon despair that man can be redeemed from himself. It is a nightmare vision which irrationally channels away much of the wealth being created, it is a neurosis to disguise from ourselves our true violence in condemning much of the world to undernourishment if not starvation.

The victims are mainly under five and offer us little resistance, certainly they have failed to wake us from the nightmare with their faint whimperings. Where enlightened self interest should be diverting this flow of vast wealth away from the munitions lines and towards developing the rest of the world, instead comes a

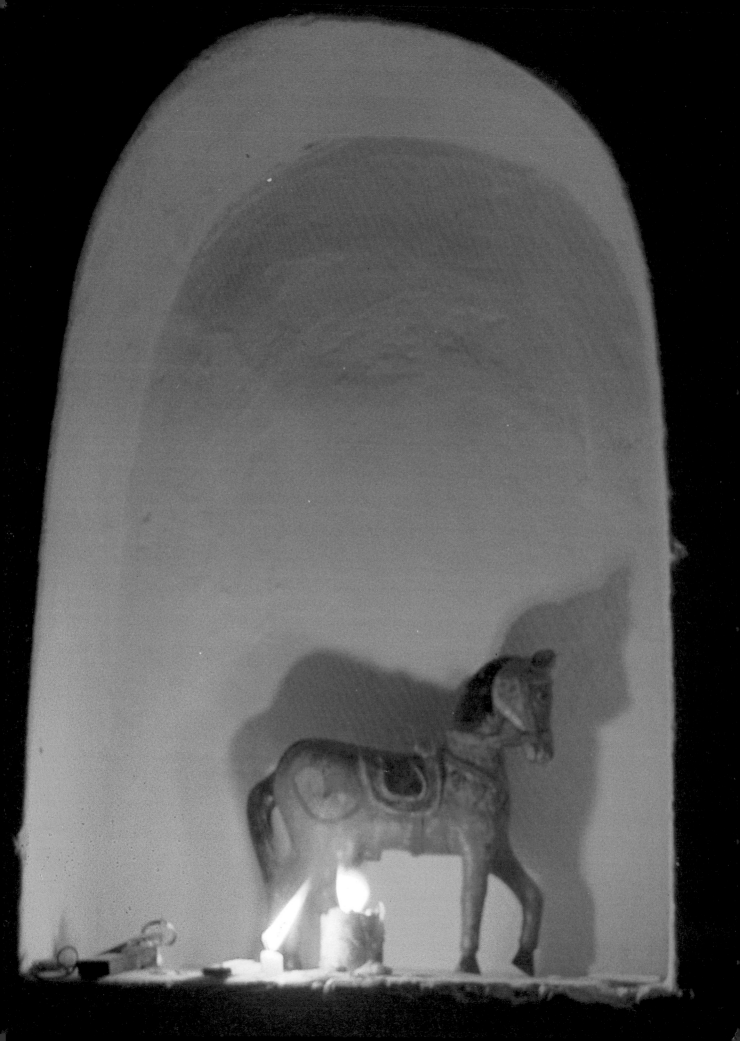

studied refusal to face reality, what is uncomfortable we think may have to be destroyed. In the meantime technology must wait for the development of the new markets which it is so capable of serving.

In rural India, the fruits of prosperity are not thrown carelessly away on the creation of a nightmare. But then rural India is not haunted by unreasonable fears and the ghosts of past evil in the same way as Europe. However, at the time of partition whole towns did fall into a bloodletting orgy where Hindu sought out Muslim and Muslim sought out Hindu to extract a terrible revenge. Yet for the Hindu, at least, tolerance of other cultures and creeds is normally that civilisation's highest achievement. And it is the unholy precedent of partition which may yet see part of the sub-continent as the first atomic battleground once Pakistan has the bomb thanks to Western connivance.

Previous page left A 100-year-old horse in a traditional Rajasthan style. In the half light it has a mythic beast quality like that of a unicorn. Magical and benign, its aura comes from the vast Asian steppes whence the Rajasthanis came as Aryan invaders with their prized form of mobility.

Previous page right Sitting at the side of a pavement in Ajmer, this man with the faraway eyes earns his living predicting the future of passers-by. Astonishingly, in spite of or perhaps because of his situation, he spoke excellent English and made several correct verifiable predictions.

Peacocks outlined against the sky in Pushkar. They, like all the animals, are used to being unmolested so that there is no real separation between human beings and the rest of creation. And, of course, the animals add their own calm to what is already a very calm town.

Celebrating the full moon

20

As happens frequently all over the Indian subcontinent, the electricity has been lost in a power cut. But on the night of the full moon the guest house on the desert fringes of Pushkar has unwittingly laid on the perfect answer to this minor inconvenience. A Rajasthani *cobratim* player has come from the village of Ghenada across the desert (with his wife) and now he settles down to play the instrument which belongs to the same family as the violin. He threads his bow across the strings and immediately in the twilight darkness conjures up all the passion and romance that comes from living in this frontier country of desert with almost perpetually clear skies. Upon his bow are tiny bells that he uses to give a tingling beat to his playing. His voice is strong and rich, even though only 20 years old, and has a haunting quality to it. He is accompanied by his wife, who is perhaps 18 or 19. Her voice is even more thrilling, full of a beseeching expressed in a perfect melody and rhythm. By the light of the log fire, the couple are both handsome and wholly Rajasthani in their quiet intensity.

Past the guest house you enter the desert. Walk along the soft sanded path and the houses simply drop away, you confront what is a winter night in the desert. On both sides are the stretching lines of blue shrouded mountains clearly seen in the moonlight which colours the sand a frosty light blue, as if it were snow. The air is perfectly fresh, so much so that each gulp of this air clears the lungs and restores a feeling of harmony. Among other things, we have forgotten how to breath deeply and rhythmically, with the result that we have become plagued by stress, a sympton of our deprivation of life-enriching air.

You walk for some time under the eerie moonlight with sharply etched shadows all about. It is fairyland you have stumbled upon, the land has a vivid welcoming presence, just as it used to have in all those childhood enchanted kingdoms. You wonder if that was indeed the message of the tales, that this is how the earth really is if we can leave behind our assorted jumble of mental luggage from the past. A building can be seen in the distance, white, many pillared with the sun's swastika sign emblazoned upon its upper portico where the flat roof begins. Directly alongside this 'moon' temple is another smaller temple that stands at the top of some steep steps leading down deep into the earth. Descend these steps and you pass out of the light of the moon into darkness until at the foot of the steps you see still water reflecting back the light of the moon. Certainly you understand why there is a temple above this life-giving water. In the grounds of the two temples is a solitary tree, a spectral presence. Seen from the roof of the temple, the mountains spread out to the horizon in magnificent disregard. It is one of those ancient sacred spots you can fall upon anywhere in India, the country's magic, which still lives.

Under the full moon light, camels can be seen slowly passing in the night, perfectly quiet with carts that run upon rubber wheels following obediently behind the stately animals. Vultures attend the corpse of a dead calf, its rear feet tied together. These birds are giant creatures even before they unfold their great wingspans at the approach of human beings and retreat a discreet distance to patiently wait.

Upon reaching Ghenada you are at last in the essential Indian

15,000 feet up in the Himalayas of Kashmir is a cave reputed to be the birthplace of Shiva. Here at this sacred site in the month of August a pilgrimage takes place to gaze upon the stalagmite which rises and falls according to season. It is reputedly Shiva's lingam.

The full moon rises at Pushkar. A time of festivity for the townspeople. Music drifts across the lake. Out in the desert the sand is silvery, a lone temple beside a well in the valley between the mountains hints at the miracle of procreation and birth amid barrenness.

village, which even the inhabitants of Pushkar venture into with caution. There are a few scattered houses about, no electricity is available because of the power cut, while the farmer has returned to using manual labour as the price of diesel has made it unprofitable to run his irrigation pumps very often. The *cobratim* player soulfully plays into the night beside the fire, while his wife ringingly answers his questioning phrases. They are telling – in all its beauty – the thousands-of-years-old story of Ram and his soulmate Sita. It is retold now with all the old passion, for these two young Indians it is the truth handed down, and the wisdom the story contains sits easily upon their straight shoulders. The epic tale confirms their rightness in being suspicious of strangers; they treat the visitor from Pushkar with as much wariness as they treat the Europeans. In the villages, there is still the old tribal code to follow, and this includes for Rajasthanis the use of force where necessary.

The man is named 'Red Grass' while his wife is called after the Pushkar lake. In the long epic they sing, they become the playful god and goddess, who for love of each other underwent many trials. They instinctively understand the message that this is how they should treat each other, as incarnations of the godhead. In the woman's lap is an 18-month old child who nestles to her warmth beside the fire.

Garsilal – 'Red Grass' – and his 19-year-old wife Kashi – Holy Water – sing the epic tale of the love of Ram and Sita around their desert encampment fire. After all manner of trials and tribulations, the couple's love overcomes misfortune. For these two desert people, the story has a truth that extends into their own lives, as they seek to model themselves on their deities. The couple earn a living singing at state fairs, where a huge 9 foot tapestry prompts them to remember all the incidents in the folk tale.

'Red Grass' proudly shows us a 9-foot-long tapestry which depicts all the incidents in his epic. He uses it to prompt him when he is singing the saga at the increasingly common folk festivals sponsored by the State tourist department. It took him 4 years to paint and is executed in a style that is both folk art and hints at the Mongol origins of the horses it depicts, they have a mythic beast quality like that of a unicorn or a dragon. In the aliveness of the creatures is a hint of the wide open Asian steppes from where both he and the Europeans once came. In Pushkar resides some of the clearest hints you will find of how our common ancestors once lived. A tough reverential life, with time enough for contemplation of the mysteries.

The Mongolian features of this head – found on a boat – hint at the various visitors who have left their mark upon India. The temples at Benares, too, hint of the linking lines with contemporaneous civilisations in Babylon and Egypt.

The women of India

21

The women of India are always present, always unobtrusively there in the background, and it is they who preserve the culture most conscientiously. They will modestly draw their saree across their face at the approach of a stranger, they are shy in front of a camera, and never let their curiosity about foreigners lead them into opening a conversation. Many are extremely pious, it shows in their calm unshadowed faces. Indeed, the tenets of Hinduism, which are now being followed less closely by the younger educated Indians, enjoin the women not to eat from sunset to sunrise, making it difficult to share a meal with working husbands you would think, and rightly so, for women are not encouraged to eat with their husband. Even though during the day they will have worked in the fields, fetched and carried, looked after children, tidied their house, all done with a tread of light grace and a perfectly straight back.

It is the men who approach any visitor to India, be they male or female. Once they have gained their confidence, women visitors will be welcomed into the giggling confidence of Indian women, even though they are rather shocking to Hindus in the way that they are constant companions to men. However, Western women in India quickly learn that they are regarded as rather inferior, being kept waiting in queques, being abruptly harassed by importuning Indian men. In response, they adopt a guarded approach to their social contacts with the tide of Indian humanity that sweeps over any visitor. Their dress becomes more modest, while they are constantly reminded that Easterners find Western women's forwardness extremely provocative – with the inevitable corollary that a woman in India, if she wishes to travel alone (and it is possible, even common now) must make sure that she does not allow herself to be alone with a man in a room. The bejeaned, casual Western dress often gives way to Indian blouses and skirts. Some, of course, shrug off the attentions of the men, and continue to dress as they do in the West.

A palmist is sitting by the roadside in Ajmer, Rajasthan. He calls out to the author, 'You are a lucky man.' Curiosity forces one to retread one's footsteps on hearing this welcome message and to sit down at the roadside in front of the turbanned, handsome man with his distant knowing eyes. The palmist speaks a Hindu form of English which is perfectly comprehensible once you have adjusted to figures of speech like, 'I see in your forehead two children.' A psychic conjuring trick is demonstrated. He tears off a piece of paper and writes upon it, without revealing what he has written.

'Think of a flower,' he says.

'A rose.'

He writes down three numbers on another piece of paper - 876.

'Pick a number.'

'Seven.'

He hands over the piece of paper he first wrote upon. On it is written in capital letters ROSE. Underneath it the number 7. He tells the author he will take an airbus ride in 5 days. Perfectly correct. It is astounding how people with these powers can be found in the oddest corners of the country. But then mental empathy is no stranger to an Indian. Wherever you go, people appear to direct and assist you, it comes from an ability to feel

Unlike most Indian women, this *sadhu* has a gracious accepting smile for all. She sits outside the gate of the Brahma temple in Pushkar and is living evidence of how Hinduism – in its teachings – lays as much stress on the female principle as on the male.

Top left Women are as devout as men in making their worship. If not more so. Having changed into a simple cotton sheet while she dipped herself in the Ganges, the woman now discreetly gets dressed again. Occasionally village women forget the all-pervading modesty they are meant to display, tribal women much more so, but India is a puritanical society.

Top middle Full of life and humour, the wife of a man who runs a tea shop on the *ghats* at Benares comes to sit and talk with some of the customers. The lower down the scale of caste, the freer a woman becomes in her social contacts, but they are still rigidly defined.

Top right Indian women marry early – in their teens. They have little time to question the prevailing social customs before they are themselves raising children in the old ways. The need for security encourages conservatism, expressed in a reluctance to mix with foreigners. The smile here is being given to a woman tourist, it would be regarded as suggestive for an Indian woman to smile at a foreign man.

empathy which cuts through mere language and race. All India is present at the same fascinating film show, each person playing his part with gusto and complete concentration.

But to return to the underlying harmony of India and the nurturers of the infrastructure – the women. In Hindu religion, women are assigned an equal place along with the male gods, in fact each god has his female consort, Vishnu, for example, the preserver and dispenser of sustenance and wealth is more worshipped through Lakshmi, his wife. While Shiva's wife, Parvati, is the essence of the female sexual energy which conjoined with that of her husband can transport a couple to transcendental delight, a healing of the body and a knowledge of the macrocosm. A concept depicted in the embrace of the yoni, with the kundalini snake of awoken energy wrapped around the transcending lingam.

At the bathing *ghats* of Benares or Pushkar, you will find the women modestly undressing to perform their ablutions in the cleansing, healing waters. Draped in a single piece of linen they intone their praises to the creator with a simple unobtrusive fervour, as they do when they place flowers upon their household shrine, or the temple shrine. Not for nothing is India spoken of instinctively as Mother India.

Temple bells ring out across the oasis of a lake that is Pushkar while all around is the arid desert, making the great expanse of water even more of a miracle. It is the night before the full moon, another hint of welcome fertility in the midst of apparent sterility. The townspeople retire early in preparation for their worshipful celebration of the moon – a female deity worshipped long before the masculine sun, but then the ways of Pushkar are old indeed. As is the calm that descends on all who visit here.

The peace of centuries lingers on in the desert oasis that is Pushkar. Almost every visitor has a soft spot for this simple, beautiful town that is still surrounded by desert. However, across the mountain range lies the busy expanding town of Ajmer, and the nearest train station.

Kaliyuga

22

In Indian cosmology this is the age of Kaliyuga – the machine age – and it will last approximately 20,000 years. It is expected to be a time of mechanisation and also of unpleasant abrupt changes.

In village India the people watch, bearing in mind the age they are entering, the antics and machinations of the politicians. They find that the taxes on petrol and diesel fuel rise so steeply that they are unable to use the mechanical pumps that provide irrigation. To get connected to the electricity supply requires the payment of *baksheesh* or a wait of many months. The farmer here is waiting to be connected still, even though a main powerline passes only a hundred yards from his house and fields. He, naturally, regards all politicians with the same jaundiced eye. The conversation moves on to a stunning disclosure. The 1974 explosion of India's atom bomb took place in the Thar desert of Rajasthan and word quickly spread among the village people of its devastating results. For three days a great cloud of dust hung over the test site, so that the sun was blotted out. Samudra, the local barber in Pushkar, says that there are stories that the Pakistanis have exploded two bombs in the last year. Remembering that the last conflict between the two nations was only 12 years before, this seems ominous news. But no. 'Equal,' says Samudra, with some pride that India was first to have the bomb.

At 26, Samudra has earnt 15,000 rupees – £1,000 – in the 7 years since he first became a barber. He runs his own shop and seems pleased with his earnings. After two miscarriages, his wife of 7 years produced a son 18 months ago. The impact produced by the arrival of many European men and women has taught him that the ways of his parents (Why are you eating with your wife?) are largely irrelevant. 'Same body,' he says, referring to men and women. 'Cut body, it bleeds, same.'

Impressed and more than a little proud of their bomb, the village masses, participants in the world's largest democracy, view from far the muddle of Indian politics. 'In America,' says Samudra, 'they have one Watergate. In India we have many. It is the way.'

But the peasants, the villagers, the small shopkeepers have their limits too. The economy's growth rate has slowed down from a spectacular 8% to a more pedestrian 4%, and they observe the foolishness of the central government with a more sceptical eye. What is astonishing is how well they understand what is taking place. 'The Indian people want no fighting,' says Samudra. 'In this age there are many wars, but not in India. We want peace.'

But politics is only a shadowy presence upon the unchanging landscape of the old India. A walk out into the desert, past the old well sunk in the earth, a man appears as if from nowhere and quickly catches you up. He engages in conversation in the inimitable Indian manner.

'Please which country? Where are you going to?'

'Buddha Pushkar.'

'My village, I show you the way.'

The man is a priest at the temple in Buddha Pushkar, an outlying village. When asked how old Pushkar is, he says 'Four yuga.' That is approximately 80,000 years. And all the time it has been a holy place, he stresses. In India there are three supremely holy places – Bodh Gaya (where the Buddha became enlightened), Varanasi and

Straight backed, strong and elegant, the power of village India radiates out from the brilliantly clad form of this woman carrying her load in the market place. Much of heavy carrying is done by women in India, on road gangs for example it is women from the villages who perform the hard labour.

Pushkar. In Pushkar, very symmetrically, there are also three holy places. One for Brahma the creator and ultimate reality, one for Shiva the destroyer and rebuilder, one for Vishnu, the preserver and bringer of prosperity. Pushkar is dedicated to Brahma and has the only temple dedicated to the creator. The priest reveals when asking for offerings after *puja* – devotions and the casting of flowers upon the waters – that there are over 500 priests in Pushkar, and that he himself at 38 has 8 children with a ninth on the way.

In the night the old presence of Pushkar pushes through more strongly. There is a quietness beside the bathing ghats at the lake so that the distant lilting call of a bird can be heard, perhaps an immigrant from Siberia. Certainly Pushkar lake offers a perfect sanctuary for any wildlife. High up on the rooftops sacred monkeys swing about. At the sight of peanuts they are willing to descend and graciously take them, but will snarl at any presumptory approach. A donkey stays by the market square all night; as he likes to listen to the music played on loudspeakers he is always to be found there. Sacred peacocks, omnipresent dogs, water buffalo, and most disconcerting of all, the quiet stately treading camels, all these are to be found gathered about the environs of the lake.

Opposite Sitting perfectly upright, an Indian child shares a mid-day meal with her father. It is the children who are being clothed in Western style, a sign that the real impact of 20th century change will affect the next generation far more than the present one.

The omnipresent lingam and yoni. Gripped by the outline of the yoni, the snake energy of Shakti flows to the lingam and in the union the lingam pierces through to achieve a mutual transcendence. How old this symbol is must be a matter for conjecture, but its worship with flowers and water suggests links with fertility cults going back 10,000 and more years. Continuity both of landscape and of civilisations is India's greatest fascination.

At the café in the morning for breakfast, there are pigeons cooing while other birds chirp in the latticework. A cow pokes its head round the wall from the adjoining stables. Women, carrying great loads of brushwood upon their heads, glint in the morning sun with their rich coloured blouses. They laugh and joke with one another in the market place. There is a sense of community, of fragrant old India.

Rajasthani men with their enormously long turbans and very solid bikes. The fastest growing form of transport besides the bicycle is the moped. Production has already reached several million a year. The present day quiet of the roads in India is about to disappear.

Opposite There are many fine handicrafts to be bought in India, pure wool shawls, elaborate jewellery, rich perfumes, exquisitely carved wooden artifacts, silks, pictures and tapestries. It is also very easy to get clothes handmade for yourself within 24 hours.

Palaces

23

Seeing India by road in either a modern bus or car is a deceptively familiar experience. The infrastructure left by the departing British still remains, little altered. Signs advising that a school or bend lies ahead, have a red triangle upon them, the traffic drives on the left and it is easy in a moment of daydreaming to imagine that you are taking a leisurely Sunday drive through a particularly rural part of Britain. Except that this is how the English countryside existed 100 years ago. You pass flocks of goats driven along the irregular tarmac edge of the road, women can be seen dotted about carrying great bundles of wood. But then you are jolted back to the present by the sheer sweep of the countryside, it is always a giant landscape, of mountains, scrub, ridges, sculpted valleys ... hinting ephemerally at its geologically recent passage through the tropics. In the south this lush tropical growth, and the unique Indian wildlife is even more plainly in evidence.

Indian townships have grown up around the routes of the old British railway network. The roads take you closer to village India, and off the roads you can enter many villages which have very little contact with the rest of the world. Here the majority of the inhabitants have thin legs, ragged clothes and seem to be covered in a perpetual layer of dust. But it is a quiet country idyll for all this. A largely pre-literate population going about living in traditional steady ways, possessed of a rhythm which has vanished from Europe within living memory, but gone completely for all that.

Roads eventually take you to towns where you re-encounter tourists from all over the world. But even in the most popular of tourist spots – such as the palaces at Udaipur, Rajasthan, or the Taj Mahal 200 miles away at Agra – you are still unforgettably in the unique Indian environment. Cows, camels and goats wander alongside the newest tourist hotels at the lakeside in Udaipur. While out in the middle of the lake a former palace has been turned into a luxury hotel which is perpetually full with both Indian and European honeymoon couples. This isolated gem is separated by only 100 yards from the rich exotic brew of Indian life. So even if you come to India for two weeks and stay at a different palace every night – there is actually a specific tour available if you are so inclined – the Indian experience will still reach through to you and stay with you alongwith the sights of fabulous architecture and exotic history. This rich texture is produced by the bulk of population living at an intensity which poverty forces upon people, they have to live in the present. And it is this intensity which will reach through to you and leave you subtly changed. It is always a shock to confront the facts of life, and those who arrive at Bombay airport and then turn around to leave again, are not isolated cases. However, the temporary suspension of Western values – if only for a few days – is rewarded by the restoring of a sense of shared humanity. The result of living among 700 million people who are direct descendants of the ancient Hindu culture.

It is, of course, entirely possible to be so bewitched by the ever changing climate and landscape that the people can pass relatively unnoticed. But the climate too is an assault upon jaded senses. In the south it stays a warm 70°F even at night in winter, while in the north it can be snowing in the Himalayan foothills and close to

The Lake Palace Hotel at Udaipur in Rajasthan is justly famous for its location in the middle of a lake. To stay the night will cost approximately £25, with booking recommended, as this is a favourite honeymoon hotel. It is also possible to visit the hotel and sip tea in surroundings that are modern and elegant, however the feel is that of a hotel not of a former palace. Less pretentious former palaces on the land carry more of their grandeur, one is actually run by the brother of a *maharajah*.

freezing at night in places like Delhi. However, the return of the sun means that the days will be warm with temperatures reaching 60°F to 70°F after even the coldest night. You will see Indians clothed in shawls and jumpers, with scarfs around their ears all day long. But for a European the Indian winter is a welcome respite and reminder that the sun still shines away from Europe. To visit India in April and May on the other hand, just before the monsoon breaks, is always a physical ordeal, for the temperature shoots up to 120°F on occasions; at such temperatures it becomes difficult to even think, however the experience of such heat has its own dazzling reality, the landscape takes on a dreamlike quality. Every movement must be carried out with the maximum of economy. Your thoughts are always on the next drink, the next cooling shower. India floats before your eyes, very obviously an entirely different place from the one you so recently left.

The old British Raj administrators solved the problem by retiring to the hills. In the north, there was Kashmir, with its fabled Dal lake and houseboats, the famous Mughal Gardens at Shalimar, still preserved much as they were, and the backdrop of the Himalayas. An ideal place to rent a house outside Srinagar and watch the sunsets in surroundings of transparent beauty. You can watch a horseman riding on the pathways that criss cross the lakes, and at sunset time be immediately transported back to the era when Mongol invaders from across the Himalayas came to this land. This heritage is in any case etched into the sharp features of the populace, with their shaved heads, their fundamentalist Muslim precepts, and their vigorous manner. (Kashmiri salesmen are among the most persistent in the world). Further to the south in Tamil Nadu there is Ootacamund in the Nilgin mountains, another favourite of the departed English. In fact, here in surroundings as lush as any in Europe it is still possible to find the last of the English living a genteel lifestyle which they have perpetuated long after it has gone from their mother country.

The Nilgiri mountains in Ooty, in the south. The land is rich and fertile and this former favourite summer home of the British retains some of that Old World charm (or desuetude depending on your orientation). However, after the heat of the plains, Ooty does offer light relief from a very physical environment during the hot months.

Opposite A *cobratim* player who will serenade you with his haunting sounds, evoking the long Rajasthani tradition of epic valour, epic loves and epic events, Rajasthan preserves one of the largest and most evocative collection of folk stories, and most of the people perform the songs as a form of worship. You have never heard music like this before.

An Indian Idyll

White sheets of still water under a half moonlight,
A land lain undisturbed for much of history,
Visited in the past by an eerie knowingness,
A discipline demanding sacrifice of all.
A beneficient place where a seeker may live
Off the bounty of Earth, find perpetual warmth
On southern shores, perpetual cold in the north.
Forests to reside in, undisturbed for seasons,
Reflecting on the purposes of the lone soul.
A method of handing on knowledge as a gift,
Earned by moral worth, borne out by experience.
In the blue of night old pathways beckon, allure.

The awakening takes place in a mountain cave.
Fifteen thousand feet above sea, approached by tracks
Threading through passes and dizzying drops; snow clad
Amarnath, birthplace of Shiva, spirit guide.
His white lingam rises and falls with the water,
A sacred place for those on the epic journey
That will lead to heaven. Come now down to the Earth,
Tread through Kashmir's vales, from some thick wooded hill tops
Watch the sun rise and then set behind blue mountains
Reflected in the lake, horsemen ride across paths,
Expert as any Mongol invader, be still
At the edge of morning water, start the day fresh.

Armies rumble through night near the shifting border,
The deep abysses of war populate dark holes,
Subterranean moves reveal their power too late.
Set off, you tread along the routes of conquerors.
Alexander, building cities, leaving the children behind.
Into the Ganges spreading plains, follow the moon's beams
To the joining of rivers, crash down from the crags.
Hardwar, the holy men appear in profusion
Watching the coming of another day from rock
Platforms, they seem as stationary as the sun
Watching the Earth turn in its orbit, a passage
Through the galaxy takes twenty four thousand years.

Dawn at the ghats in Benares comes like a shock.
Behind the trees on the vast plain, the sun appears
Illuminating the wide Ganga with orange
Rays, by the time it is an hour old temple priests
Are dispensing waters upon many lingam
Shrines set in alcoves in the temple walls, above.
The hubbub of pilgrims below dipping away
Their sins in ritual. The priest moves slowly, booms
'Om Shiva' at the gates of the temple, moves on
To the shrine of Parvati, as strong as her man
In the charge of energy that starts from below
And heads on its course to the very upper crown.

The moon grows daily, now it is seen above sea,
The warmed seas of the south, where the foreigners came
Putting an end to self mastery that had lived
Unchanged from the time of the Buddha, first preaching
Lessons some few miles from the Ganga at Sarnath.
But the palms on the southern shores sway, unresisting
The call of the moon while there is any sign of life.
Death for the ancient sea turtle, at the sea's edge
Its flippers idly ply the tide as if it were alive.
The birds have perceived its motionlessness, flock to peck
the cold flesh, by the return of the next moon night
only shell form, the same for millions of years.

The narrow passageways of Benares keep out
Those who have not grown up in labryrinths of cows,
Dogs, goats, donkeys and caged birds. Cool in heat of day,
At dusk they hide a multitude of secret learning,
The horoscopes are cast in the ancient Sanskrit way.
In tatters, the meanings of the calculations.
Philosophers muse on the sacred Vedic texts
Musicians practise at the feet of old masters.
A man must follow a path to its conclusion,
Aware of the arrivals for burning on logs
Must use his time well, until he has become free,
Master of a tune in harmony with the past.

Midnight at the circle of hills in kingly Rajgir
Where the Buddha spent years wandering and teaching,
The home of the magnificent Ashoka who
Used Gautama's laws and ensured a lasting peace.
Even now in its decline the temples on peaks,
White and remote, guard the peace of the lush valley.
At its soft centre a shrine to the snake goddess,
The feminine knows the earth's magic, while stones guard
The memory of one who passed among them once.
At the caves are left traces of early teachers,
The air is still charged with an electric current
That instantly transmits the mystery of man.

The thunderbolts of Himalayan storms echo
Over Kathmandu, olden city of temples,
People stay in their homes, dwarfed by the whitened peaks.
Animals may be sacrificed to appease deities,
Tibetans who fled down from the high plateau
Say their prayers upon wheels that turn in the cold wind,
Sacred monkeys clamber, watched by the all seeing eye
Of the temple, the symbol of a thunderbolt
Perfectly frames a gap in encircling mountains
Through which pour the dispensers of Tibet's magic
With knowledge of the coming cycle for the world,
Their faces eagle sharp, kind, keeping some distance.

A perfect day in the village of Bodh Gaya,
The ageing sadhu moves like an Indian ram,
Yet pauses to bless the worth of the bullock
Endlessly turning circles as it grinds the corn,
Fruits and flowers, the choicest of the Earth's bounty
Find their way upon leaves to their recipients,
Fragrant old India takes her repast and thanks
The Earth for nurturing all that lives, that exists
To surpass itself and turn from one lakeside flower
Into a hundred equally dazzling pure shapes.
At the pool's side the two lovers who have lain on
A carpet of grass smile wordlessly with their love.

The desert at the time of full moon, Brahma's home,
A clear lake has gathered about it small white shrines,
Bells chime in night, the expanses of the chill blue
Wastes of sand call out, here there is the breathing Earth,
Steep sided mountains surrounding the desert track,
A white pillared, flat topped temple and alongside
A deep sunken well reached down shadowed steep sheer steps.
At their foot, still waters reflecting the moon,
Glinting with an old light, the food for life it is,
A solitary tree, Shiva and Shakti make
An embrace that powers with the moon into a burst
Of thousands of seeds upon the barren empty ground.

The perfectmost creation, thus has Pushkar stood
For four journies around the hub of the galaxy,
Calm flows out from waters whistled upon
By birds and geese who have flown here from distant lands
To join the bright natives in their emerald greens,
Over the heads of teeth baring monkeys who take
What is given without losing sense of danger
From the trickery of man. Cows meander streets
Snuffling into roots heaped upon the ground for them,
Birds in the latticework chirp, pigeons coo deeply
Beside the lake, while in the deep waters great fish
Twist round the grasses that grow at the water's edge.

The epics are retold by each generation,
The bomb that sent dust clouds into the sky for days
Reminds of the almighty power, peace must be won
The singers sing behind the haunting cobratim
With a sound to carry across desert spaces.
All is free, as it should be when you have crossed
The desert, worshipped at the last temple then found
Communion and eventually come to gaze
Upon the coming dawn with a marvelling awe.
Beauty astounds, is cast out by an angry mind
Trying to change what it cannot change or improve.
Death comes, the old Sadhu leaves to a wedding march.

Love and marriage, sex and censorship

'The woman should ever strive to close and constrict the yoni *until it holds the* lingam *as with a finger, opening and shutting at her pleasure, and finally, acting as the hand of the Gopi girl, who milks the cow. This can only be learned by practice, and especially by throwing the power of the will into the part to be affected. This art, once learned, is never lost. Her husband will then value her above all women, nor would he exchange her for the most beautiful queen. So lovely and pleasant to man is she who can constrict her* yoni *in this way.'* **Ananga Ranga**

Although that favourite Indian god, Krishna, is depicted as happily frolicing with *Gopis* (cow girls) in calendar pictures, present day India has a far less free and easy attitude to relationships between the sexes. Public display of affection is rarely seen, and if a white woman kisses her boyfriend in public the looks will be as fascinated as if the couple were engaged in the full act of love. Kissing has recently escaped the film censor's scissors in the 3-hour long sagas portrayed by Indian films. Pert, provocative women and jocular, rather paunchy male stars put together good song and dance acts. Out there in the villages, the market for Bombay's huge film industry (it is one of the few sources of income for Westerners, they can sometimes act as extras) this is how they would like life to be. Charming, vivacious girls who show their winning, flashing smiles to men who only wish to charm and court them, the dance being the culmination of the relationship. Yet in the outlying villages they do indeed dance and sing and smile. Not as often as on the cinema screen it is true, but it is still the true heart of India where *joie de vivre* lives on. A life modelled on the happy ways of gods and goddesses.

The Westernised press has started to publish pictures of pin-ups but it is an aberration, a picture of Lakshmi or Parvati is far more likely to win an Indian's heart. Meanwhile the old marriage customs continue unabated.

Nearly all Indian husbands do not see their bride more than once before the marriage day. The couple are matched by the parents. Whatever claims are made for the wisdom of this method, a perusal of the advertising columns of *The Times of India*, for example, will reveal that caste, money and age are the all important determinants. The astrologers will be consulted for their approval, but the rooting of marriage in the passing on of family wealth has produced a very fixed order. A girl is expected to bring a reasonable dowry to the husband and even modest families are required to settle 20,000 to 30,000 rupees (£1,400–£2,000) on their daughters. Sometimes the money is paid in instalments, and failure to pay is ground enough for divorce.

Even 26-year-old master tabla player, Kasho Rao Nayak, who has recorded in Japan and spends some 4 months of each year there, went along with his father's choice of a 19-year-old girl with no interest in music. The comparison of their astrological charts said that it would be a successful union. After marriage she moved into her father-in-law's house and alongwith the five brothers and two sisters of her husband, she became part of the family. She is not encouraged to see her own family, except when the first born arrives and her own mother is consulted on childcare.

Pushkar barber, Bal Mukand, claims the system produces much

The Indian ideal of modern beauty as evinced by a shop mannequin. The mark between the eyebrows is the location of the 'third eye' of spiritual insight but the mark is now worn to show a woman is married.

unhappiness — with so much money involved, a divorced girl would be almost excluded from society unless her parents could find an even more handsome dowry the second time around. Bal says there are a suspicious number of kerosene explosions in kitchens with the wife dying, two or three are reported in the paper each week. But then he also claims that ruthless husbands sell their wives to the tourists for 10 rupees a night and that is certainly a product of his fevered imagination. Women simply do not come into contact with Westerners, although a friendly Tibetan is quite capable of offering his wife to a visitor as a gesture of friendship. India, however, is not Tibet.

Indian prurience means that any Western woman is going to be treated as a film star while she is there, it is so unusual for the men to be able to speak freely to a woman who is outside the strict Hindu code. Unlike many countries of a Muslim persuasion, she is fairly free of the threat of rape, the Indian works more on the principle of wearing down objections. And it is here in this elemental meeting of East and West that the differences and prejudices are proved to be as strong as ever. From the Indian side just as much as from the European.

Although many tourists bathe nude in Goa, it is not officially condoned. Occasionally the local police will visit the beaches urging people to cover themselves, some argue, some simply don their swimming costumes until the police disappear. It all has an air of unreality to it in a country surrounded by such pressing problems.

All this is something of a travesty of the old Hindu culture, where women were allowed and expected to take a full public role. At the time of the Mughal invasions in the 16th century, the Indians had to hide their women away to save them from molestation. And this tradition has continued right through until today.

'The two participants should meet each other halfway. Then the encounter becomes a feast.'
From an Eastern novel of 200 years ago.

Opposite The 19-year-old wife of master table player, Kesho Rao Nayak, who is 26. Although she is obviously quite happy she does not come across to greet her husband's visitors unless invited. The segregation of the sexes in India continues after marriage.

In the cities you will find advertisements advising that 'two is enough', but for many Indians the family is their only protection in old age. Hence, forced vasectomy programmes notwithstanding, the population continues to grow.

Invest in National Savings Certific

PROTECT YOUR FAMI

The Taj

26

It has been called the most beautiful temple in the world. Even though built at the cost of much human life, the white marbled mausoleum at Agra has become the monument of a man's love for a woman.

In 1631 when his wife died in childbirth, the emperor Shah Jahan brought to Agra the most skilled craftsmen from all Asia and even Europe. He intended to build a black marbled mausoleum for himself and link the two by a silver bridge. But the enemy of mortality stopped this breathtakingly beautiful conception.

Everyone has their own favourite time to see the Taj Mahal. Crowds will distract you from the coolly serene presence of this flawless monument. Try arriving just as it opens or is about to close. A few minutes alone in the perpetually echoing inner sanctum will reward you far more than several hours spent on a guided tour. The sensuously curving lines of the temple of love demand to be savoured without interruption, then the presence of the building itself will impart its own message.

The tombs of Shah Jahan and his wife Mumtaz Mahal are actually located in a shadowy burial crypt. At ground level, in the very centre of the building is the cenotaph dedicated to Mumtaz. Sing in this inner shrine and the notes will float upwards in a presentiment of the music of the spheres.

Relax and be open. Under a full moon the pearly white exterior is shrouded in mystery. Love, the greatest mystery of all. In India, part at least of your time will be spent learning and gaining new perspectives. That lasts.

Opposite The Taj at midday. Each hour of each day has its own mood reflected in the white tiles of the mausoleum. Try to visit at twilight when the whole of the surrounding countryside is suffused in the intense glow of an Indian sunset. Few people come away from Agra unimpressed.

Delicate graceful flowers, just one of the thousands of exquisite touches that distinguish the Taj from all other buildings. The finest craftsmen in the world were brought to Agra for the ultimate memorial to a woman's love.

The Kaleidoscope

27

Anyone who comes to India is changed, and the longer your stay the greater the change. A distance creeps into the expression, together with an expanded knowledge of the world's beauties and woes. Above all, there is a freedom in the country to experience life in all its manifestations. It is better to commit these impressions to the memory while they are fresh for, inevitably, once back in the West, the old preconceptions about the starving, disease-wracked Indians dominate the thinking, quite leaving out the beauty, comforting culture and rich religion which fortify the people's lives.

What will your stay be like? Like nothing you imagined. For in India events happen to you which seem to elucidate what it is you are really seeking within yourself. It is, most of all, a spiritual country, even though the spirit is constantly abused by a ruling class that is even more remote from the mass of people than the British were. In addition, the rulers and bureaucrats are far less scrupulous about honesty and fair dealing, a world weariness consumes the politicians so that the people will turn now to a film star, later a religious fanatic. The old rulers are largely discredited.

But behind this surface chaos there is a thrust towards making the country self-reliant, an aim almost all Indians would agree to. Any amount of casualties along the way are accepted. So a space programme is pursued at a cost of millions of pounds, armaments are bought in increasing numbers in preparation for war. It is the irony of Hindu society that theirs is a land where exceptionally cruel wars have been fought when the precious peace breaks down. There is a gloating cruelty in the way that rich Indians can look through a leper standing beside their expensive car, and an underlying philosophy that the poor will always be with us. Quite unlike China across the border.

So the beggar children of Bombay will importune a Westerner for many minutes in preference to trying to elicit sympathy from their own people. However, it is good for a Westerner to come face to face with the reality of the East/West conflict.

Most will find a defence in saying that the Indians should learn to look after themselves. Have no fear, it is precisely this ruthless logic that the young are learning and the future can only hold out the prospect of a bitter struggle for economic power between the East and West, North and South.

But it is the India of spices, fabulous stones, ancient temples with ever more shadowy inner rooms, dusty *sadhus*, massive sweeping countryside, life in all its profusion, that is the heart of the land.

It can be sampled on many levels and each will have its vivid immediacy. One minute you are unwittingly talking to a prince in his former palace turned into an hotel, the next you are bargaining over whether the cost of a lengthy taxi ride should be 50 pence or 75 pence. A bargaining session you will enter into with gusto as the reality of a far lower standard of living seeps through to you.

Travel on trains and buses will be as fascinating as the destination, and will always take longer than you anticipated. Allow up to 4 hours for lateness on day-long journies, breakdowns and delays occur all along the line or road.

Whether your interest is in bringing back some of the exotic

Opposite An extraordinary rock relief to be found at Mahamalla Puram, some 30 miles south of Madras. Well over 1,000 years old, it depicts gods, human beings and animals in peace and meditation.

The local Goan people do not find nudity a problem, traders approach the sunworshippers as energetically as ever, even women traders will carry on selling their wares to naked men unconcernedly. However, middle-class Indians make bus trips simply to see the sights.

perfumes, statues, clothes or jewellery; in reliving the old rural lifestyle; in finding a fresh purpose and vividness to life; in searching out a teacher or *guru* in some ancient discipline; in seeing lush nature and teeming animal life (India is well along the way to protecting much of its wildlife); you are entering a way of life both far more ancient and far more changing than our relatively fixed lifestyles permit us. This is an experience worth having – at least once in your short life.

Previous page The magic of an Indian dawn. The intensity of the light in India is wholly different from that of Europe, and brings a drama to the opening of any day that has to be experienced to be understood.

Cautionary tales and helpful hints

28

The unexpected is to be expected in India, but a little forewarning of some of the surprises which could lie in wait will do much to assuage the anxiety you may feel about your visit.

Taken at random and starting with health here are some simple tips: The water is usually fit for drinking if it comes from a tap. But be warned, especially when travelling in country districts, that the tempting glass of water on your table probably comes from a well and is suspect. If in doubt, drink the ubiquitous and wholly Indian sweet-tasting tea — *chai*. Eating meat is always a risk in India, refrigeration is scarcely known. In summer, eating meat is an invitation to a bloated stomach, a common occurrence which can be relieved by pills from a pharmacy.

Any cuts need to be treated immediately. Many Europeans are slow to heal in the heat until their bodies have adjusted to the new conditions and food. Penicillin ointments can be bought over the counter at pharmacies, but the best way to help the body is to eat local foods where possible. Never eat cooked food which has been allowed to cool, follow your nose, a café or restaurant which is giving off a bad smell is no place to stop. In India you ignore your health at high cost, as is testified all around you. Be thankful if you don't get a stomach upset in the first two or three weeks, after that you can become a little more experimental with the food. Eating yogurt daily helps to ward off unfriendly bacteria.

The snake, worshipped as a symbol of the energy the female can release, is also the bringer of sudden death to 8,000 Indians a year. The discovery of one, under a stone perhaps, will cause mayhem in an Indian village until it is killed.

It is possible to buy an Indian-made motor cycle for remarkably little and Europeans who are staying some months quickly become enthusiasts for the old-style models available. The un-European possibility of riding down largely empty roads still exists but speeding is not recommended for anything could lie around the next corner.

Previous page A brilliantly dressed Rajasthani woman in the market place. Although the women are on the streets just as much as the men, they keep themselves in the background, sometimes sitting almost the whole day in the same position.

Opposite A woman sweeps the steps at Benares. A lowly occupation but perhaps an enlightening one. The author spoke to a former university professor turned *sadhu* who did this for a living in Benares. 'You people, living like kings in our city,' he good-humouredly jibed. India is like that.

Get all the immunisation shots you can. The really dangerous infection to watch out for is rabies. If you are bitten by a dog and suspect it is rabid (after two days incubation, during which time it is still infectious, rabies produces strange behaviour in dogs) you need to go to a hospital immediately for preventative shots. Once rabies takes hold it will very probably kill.

You are unlikely to be the victim of robbery with violence in India but beware of quick fingers and trickery. Wear a money belt. Carry cash and travellers cheques in two separate places. Keep a note of the cheque numbers and make sure the cheque company has branches in at least the major cities. Beware of black market money changers in the street — they are liable to suddenly hiss 'police' and push a bundle of notes into your hand before they disappear with your money — and a fat profit. Carry a padlock for securing your room or bag.

Dormitory-type accommodation is always the most at risk. Some of your fellow travellers could be desperate for funds. If you are stuck, your consulate will help to get money sent out or send you back home with your passport used as surety for repayment.

Don't take more clothing and gear than you absolutely need. Many of the items you want to take can be bought very cheaply once you arrive. (Some people even buy Indian motor bikes). There is no fun in humping round a huge rucksack filled with possessions that simply serve to bolster your imaginary sense of 'security'. Also, you will probably want to bring home some of the handicrafts you will be offered almost daily. (Large items like Tibetan carpets in Kathmandu can be very efficiently sent by post).

Always bargain over price. Take as a rough guide that the first price asked is anywhere between 25% and 200% over the real one. You will need patience, an Easterner will happily bargain over a period of days. The best guide is what a selection of fellow travellers have paid. Most deals are clinched after you have 'walked out' the door — you have to be something of an actor.